Pastors at RISK

Pastors at RISK

Protecting Your Future
Guarding Your Present

Dr. Charles A. Wickman

NEW YORK

Pastors at RISK
Protecting Your Future Guarding Your Present

© 2014 Dr. Charles A. Wickman.

Published in New York, New York, by Morgan James Publishing. Morgan James and The Entrepreneurial Publisher are trademarks of Morgan James, LLC. www.MorganJamesPublishing.com

The Morgan James Speakers Group can bring authors to your live event. For more information or to book an event visit The Morgan James Speakers Group at www.TheMorganJamesSpeakersGroup.com.

FREE eBook edition for your existing eReader with purchase

PRINT NAME ABOVE

For more information, instructions, restrictions, and to register your copy, go to **www.bitlit.ca/readers/register** or use your QR Reader to scan the barcode:

ISBN 978-1-63047-046-3 paperback
ISBN 978-1-63047-047-0 eBook
ISBN 978-1-63047-049-4 hardcover
Library of Congress Control Number:
2013955194

Cover Design by:
Rachel Lopez
www.r2cdesign.com

Interior Design by:
Bonnie Bushman
bonnie@caboodlegraphics.com

In an effort to support local communities, raise awareness and funds, Morgan James Publishing donates a percentage of all book sales for the life of each book to Habitat for Humanity Peninsula and Greater Williamsburg.

Get involved today, visit
www.MorganJamesBuilds.com

Habitat for Humanity
Peninsula and Greater Williamsburg
Building Partner

To Honor

Alvin Kimel, Sr., and Ninon Kimel

who love Pastors and Pastor-In-Residence, Inc.

Table of Contents

At-Risk And Forced Exit: An Overview

Elijah sat alone under the lone broom tree, collapsed, exhausted and wanting to die (1 Kings 19:4, 5). He was frightened; he ran to escape his tormentor; he lost his sense of personal worth (vv. 3, 4). His pain was not unlike the pain felt by hundreds of pastors on Monday after a bad Sunday. Some pastors live most of the time under the juniper tree (King James Version), exhausted, wanting to run, with little sense of personal worth. They are at risk of losing effectiveness and eventually their position as pastor. This condition drives this book.

Scores of exited pastors, puzzled and confused, have said to me, "I never saw it coming." At risk, but seemingly unaware of what in life and work put their ministry in jeopardy. Therefore, they never considered what action can and should be taken to protect their future and guard their present. In some cases, their churches were prospering but the prosperity blinded them to what repeated experience shows, that it only takes three to four percent of a congregation, even in fairly healthy churches, to force the departure of a pastor. (Particularly associate and assistant pastors.) The at-risk factors leading to forced resignation may inform the "I never saw it coming" exited pastor. This surprising blindness as to why exit happens also drives this book.

"We had to get shed of our preacher." That is how people in rural North Carolina put what we now call "forced resignation" or "involuntary separation." Hundreds of churches "get shed of the preacher" every month. While you read this book, ten pastors will be fired, two every hour. Sometimes messy. Sometimes decently and in order. But terminated nonetheless. And he is left to try to rebuild his shattered life, broken and bleeding, often as abandoned as a ghost town.

Risk can be either a benefit or a threat. Derived from the early Italian word *risicare*, it means "to dare." I'm writing about risk as threat, called "At risk." I attempt to identify the factors that put a person in Christian ministry in jeopardy of losing his confidence, self-respect, and most of all his position as pastor to his congregation.

Risk happens given the premise that we are not to be passive about the task committed to God's people. Jesus told His people "Go into all the world…" and that world was not an altogether friendly place where they could anticipate the towns they visited would hold parades in their honor and kill the fatted calf to feed them. Jesus sent His twelve disciples out "like sheep among wolves." While all men would hate them, He said, "He who stands firm to the end will be saved." While it can be argued that there is no risk in total obedience to Christ, to the disciples it surely felt like risk. Risk is part of what it means to be in ministry. No one argues against risk.

As applied to vocational pastoral ministry, being at risk has in it any number of factors and conditions, real or perceived, generally attributed to the pastor who serves a given congregation and, for a great variety of reasons and feelings, is unacceptable to it. I identify some of those factors considered primary.

To lessen the risks, here is counsel, simple, practical and appropriate to each factor. You guard the present and protect your future in ministry by knowing what puts a pastor at risk and what can lead to an unplanned loss of ministry. This is an incredible journey we are on... let us keep it that way.

The pain of a forced exit is a wound that never fully heals. My friend and colleague, Dr. Jim Krames, has put it this way:

- He feels "sucker-punched" by those he had dedicated his life and training to serve. He's doubly wounded as his pain was intentionally inflicted by friendly fire.
- Weekly, he returns to a similar church scene to watch others perform roles denied him.
- Like a victim in a vicious divorce, he lives with flashbacks of good times, and the nagging worry for those spiritual offspring he was forced to leave behind.
- Ugly showdown scenes replay in his brain, including some he can only imagine because he was not present—secret meetings where gossipers raked him over the coals.
- He feels like a fool, therefore, avoids, like the plague, every offer of counsel and companionship to help him deal with the pain, angst, and emotional bile.
- He must find a new job, but since his ministry-specific training limits his resume's marketability in the commercial world, low-paying employment looms dead ahead.
- He is constantly under surveillance by detractors for signs of bitterness. Their goal: use evidence to build a case "proving" his ouster was warranted.

The forced exit of pastors happens for a variety of reasons. Generally it is not over doctrinal issues (though moral issues such as the right to life and theological issues such as the work of the Holy Spirit sometimes divide a church and put a pastor at risk). A pastor most often loses his position over control issues. But at times it has in its construct simply a diminishing respect for leaders. At times it occurs simply because of a general tendency toward short tenures in some denominations. It has been blamed on the church growth movement with its emphasis on what does not happen in some churches, i.e., growth. When the lay leadership announces a pastor's termination, the most often "reason" given (and I've heard it SO often) is "Your gifts do not fit with what we need right now." Some live at risk even though it could lead to a forced exit, out of a "need" to live that way. *Time* magazine, in its March 8, 2008, issue, shows pictures of eight male political figures including several presidents who took high personal risks while in office. Accompanying the photographs is an article reciting studies that in terms of risk tolerance, body chemistry played a part. The article is entitled: "The Science of Risk-Taking: Why smart people do reckless things." Are some pastors programmed to and intentionally live at risk?

Pastors themselves leave ministry because their understanding of the call to ministry changes or because they need a moratorium or are unable to relocate when it seemed to them that a move was becoming necessary. Some leave because of feelings of personal inadequacy as a church leader or because their personal expectation of being successful never develops.

The question remains: Why, When, and to Whom does <u>forced resignation</u> happen? The answer is in what is called "pastors at risk." Before termination came conditions putting the pastors in jeopardy, danger, and allowing them to be vulnerable. Call "at risk" the probability of loss or exposure to the chance of loss. The loss is a loss of confidence, self-respect, trust, energy, security and ultimately the loss of vocational ministry. Thus it also becomes the loss of finances, friends and often family.

Pastors have been at risk and driven from their pulpits for decades. Recently I learned of two forced exits in the early 1800s. John Paxton, a Presbyterian minister in Virginia inherited slaves from his wife's father. While arranging for them to be sent back to Africa, he urged his congregation to free the seventy slaves owned by the church and hired out to pay the pastor's (his) salary. What he promoted so vigorously provoked the church and community that they forced him to leave the church for an Illinois parish.

In another similar situation, George Bourne advocated the expulsion of slaveholders from the church and for that he was forced to leave his Virginia pulpit.

I can only imagine that hundreds of morally courageous pastors advocating freedom for all slaves put themselves at risk and many departed their churches under duress over that issue. They were heroic pastors. Research shows that a pastor is at risk now, however, not generally over such moral issues, but when one or more of the following elements are present:

- Vision Conflict
- Compassion Fatigue
- Role Confusion
- Unclear Expectations
- Isolation and Loneliness
- Spouse and Family Unhappy
- Waning Ability to Trust Church Leadership
- Unhealthy Staff Relationship
- No Support Team
- Inadequate Church Finances
- No or Very Few Close Friends
- Overworked
- Plateaued or Declining Church Attendance

- Moral or Ethical Failure, Sometimes Not True
- Cannot Say "No"
- Inability to Meet Peoples' Needs
- Sense of Futility Reflected in his Work
- Serving a High Risk, Dysfunctional Church
- Lowered Self-esteem and a Diminished Sense of Confidence
- Trust of Denominational Leadership Weakening
- Have to Prove Self a Hard Worker
- Matters of Self-care and Self-discipline Neglected
- Not Prepared With Needed Skills
- Emotionally Empty
- Doubt About a Call to Ministry

Currently, an eight-member study group of professional Christian psychologists and others are studying the at-risk condition. Six to seven retreats of at-risk pastors will be held to hear face to face what stresses make up the at-risk experience of pastors. The results will be published.

Other factors could be added, unique to the denomination in which a pastor serves. Some factors are particular to a church's history or cultural setting. This book considers factors considered to be the *primary elements* of the at-risk condition.

The Pastor's Institute of Indiana did a study of what former pastors said impacted their leaving ministry, forced or otherwise. The study was supported by a grant from the Louisville Institute. These former pastors said they were ill- prepared, not well connected, did not see to matters of self-care and self-discipline, accepted a call to a dysfunctional church, couldn't afford to continue pastoring, not able to resolve conflict and simply lost their way.

In a survey of ninety-nine active pastors, I asked about the top stressors in ministry. The major stresses, according to these pastors, are feeling they can't meet all the needs of their people, feeling emotionally exhausted, difficulty saying "no," being overworked and generally exhausted, more expectations than can be fulfilled, isolation and loneliness, not as many close friends as they desire and the need to prove themselves hard workers.

Here are some disturbing numbers compiled by Shiloh Place (shilohplace.org/crisisin.htm):

- 70 percent of pastors constantly fight depression.
- 80 percent of pastors and 84 percent of their spouses feel unqualified and discouraged in their roles.
- 50 percent are so discouraged that they would leave the ministry if they could, but they have no other way to make a living.
- 80 percent of adult children of pastors surveyed have had to seek professional help for depression.
- 90 percent of pastors said their seminary or Bible school training did only a fair-to-poor job preparing them for ministry.
- 85 percent said they are tired of dealing with problem people.
- 90 percent said the hardest thing about ministry is dealing with uncooperative people.
- 70 percent feel grossly underpaid.
- 80 percent of pastors' wives feel left out and unappreciated by church members.
- 90 percent said ministry was completely different from what they thought it would be like before they entered ministry.
- 70 percent felt called of God to pastoral ministry before their ministry began, but after three years of ministry, only 50 percent still felt called.

Being at risk and being forced to resign are both multi-determined. Hopefully, pastors reading this book will identify the conditions that may well become the tipping points that result in the loss of their vocation.

One disturbing fact is that an at-risk pastor can harm his congregation. A dysfunctional pastor reflects his pathology in his teaching/leading function and can create a distorted faith particularly in young and weak members of his congregation. This adds to the seriousness of the at-risk phenomenon.

Disturbing also is that a pastor out of vocational ministry does not easily recover. Nearly 40 percent never return to ministry. Michael, in the movie of the same name, said about pastors in recovery: "To give a man back his heart is the hardest mission on earth." Loss is painful still; memories haunt him; hope has weakened. From years of experience I say, for a pastor to recapture his heart lost in a forced resignation is difficult, almost beyond description. Avoid it like the plague. If you are at risk, take steps now to remedy it.

CONCLUSION

A pastor has been called and committed to the greatest job in the world. He has become a pastor not to make money but to make a difference. It is a terrible thing to lose one called and committed to such a task. What I write is my experience of twenty years, much of that time also serving as a pastor. It is simple, I know, and only the counsel of one pastor to another. But a hope beats in my heart as well as the hearts of dozens of others who work to restore at-risk and exited pastors to full-time, full impact ministry. That hope is that somehow the at-risk road leading to exodus will become, to use Scott Peck's phrase, "A Road Less Traveled."

Introduction

"At a very critical time in my life and ministry, when I was hurting, I fell back into the gentle arms of friends…" Jim had been in ministry for eight years. Now he was out, with no place to go.

Conflict in the church drove him to the loss of ministry. He and his wife were devastated, angry, lonely, confused. But they had gentle friends.

"My pastor friends wrote me off as a failure," agonized one bright associate pastor. "People even suspected some great moral lapse." He resigned for reasons of personal integrity. Falsely accused, he could do no other.

Another pastor had failed God and his congregation. After repentance came restoration but he was in need of accountability, support and a place to start again someday. He needed to understand what had put him at risk of moral failure in the first place.

"I'm almost spooked by the number of people who have asked me lately when I was going to get back into ministry," said my friend, a one-time church leader, divorced and alone. "But now, how?" he asked, as if there was no answer to that question.

It was that latter remark that got me started. I had felt many of the fears pastors experience. I had bled with the best and worst of them. Proved myself a hard worker. Please everyone! Conflict over how the work of the church was to be done! Feelings of inadequacy. Those horrible parking lot meetings after church. I knew they were talking about me. If not, I was paranoid and that was about as paralyzing as if they were. Up. Down. Yes! No! Depressed, fighting mad. A veritable emotional roller coaster. I was well trained, a good pastor, I thought. Was I one of those pastors called "at risk"?

A deacon once called me "a little tin god." At that I almost quit. Twice I was to do so for non-pastoral ministry. I did my Doctor of Ministry work on exited pastors. Maybe I was in search of answers for myself. "Heroic Helplessness," Shirley Holzer Jeffrey calls it.

The church I served responded with an individually tailored program, hopeful of assisting exited pastors return to their divine calling. We call it Pastor-in-Residence. For twenty years I've cried with, counseled with and got pastors into that simple recovery program. Dozens of exited pastors have returned to vocational ministry.

Another phenomenon has haunted me, however. Fifteen hundred pastors leave their posts each month with no other place to go. (So the commonly held statistics say.) Is there no way to cut this number, even by a few dozen? There must be!

Yet another surprise to me has been that forced resignation often happens so quickly and with the pastor so unaware that he was at risk of it happening. Most pastors are not naïve. Most exited pastors, however, tell me that their "involuntary separation" was totally unexpected.

Pastors At risk: Guarding your Present, Protecting your Future gathers together what I have learned from dozens of conversations with at-risk and exited pastors. What I have written are simple answers (deliberately so), shared with pastors looking for ways to avoid being forced out of vocational ministry.

"I had no idea ministry could be this turbulent," said one stunned elder. He had just seen a demythologized sketch of the pressures and pains of ministry unfold, as an exited pastor so intensely felt them and so clearly expressed them. That night I felt understood as the same elder said to me, "Pastor, we are never going to let this happen to you." That night I knew I wasn't at risk. That night I knew that one purpose for my life was to be a friend to pastors in stress.

Struggling? Frustrated? Thinking about quitting? Hiding a confused mind behind a professional mask? Scared? This book is designed to keep you out of the statistics.

Note: Between each chapter you will read a story of an at-risk or exited pastor. For the most part these are real people, people with whom I've worked, telling their unhappy stories in their own words. A few are "composite characters," created out of my experience with dozens of troubled pastors over these past twenty years.

CHAPTER 1

Burnout: Who, What And Where Do You Go From Here?

"Seventeen percent of all pastors are at any one time burned out."
—Alban Institute

"Rob (not his real name) is the pastor of a thriving church," writes my friend Dr. Albert Els. He has invested twelve years in building it. One day he called Al to say he couldn't hold it together any more. He confessed to a hard time praying and that he was beginning to feel that preaching was not worth it anymore.

He felt overwhelmed, anxious most of the time and unable to sleep well. He couldn't concentrate like he wanted to and dreaded even returning phone calls. Later he confessed to dialing 1-900 numbers.

Jan, his wife, complained that he was irritable with her and the children. He gets upset with the elders when they ask him to change. They complain about his administrative style and his lack of consulting with them about church matters. Jan, too, was struggling with her own increased pressures and responsibilities in the church.

Diagnosis: The beginnings of burnout. Like 80 percent of pastors surveyed by Focus on the Family, discouraged and depressed, suffering fatigue and frustration. "Compassion Fatigue," as Dr. Arch Hart calls it. A sense of failure, a feeling of exhaustion, a loss of strength and energy, withdrawal from responsibilities, avoidance of other people, belief that you are no longer effective as a pastor, inner emptiness, lowered resistance to disease, all brought on by devotion to helping people or by a relationship gone bad.

Herbert Freudenberger, who coined the term "burnout," defined it as "a state of fatigue or frustration brought out by a devotion to a cause, a way of life, or a relationship that failed to produce the expected rewards." In *Burnout: The High Cost of High Achievement,* he writes [Burnout is] "a problem born of good intentions. The people who fall prey to it are, for the most part, decent individuals who have striven hard to reach a goal."

Burnout is an erosion of the soul. It is energy turned to exhaustion, compassion turned to anger, satisfaction turned to cynicism. It is devotion sans moderation, service beyond ordinary duty, work without rest, numerous downloads with no deleting.

It should be noted that the church has noticeably changed in recent years, not fitting the traditional model with which many pastors are most familiar (dance, orchestras and/or drums, drama, reader's theatre, etc.). Pastors are also experiencing highly charged competitive pressure from growing mega-churches. Technology (computers, I-pods, Power Point®, etc.), unfamiliar to older pastors, is SOP in contemporary churches. Traditional pastors are a mismatch for many such churches. Burnout may be the result of being traditional and attempting or feeling the need to be contemporary.

Some burned-out people are lethargic while others, in neurotic frenzy, work all the time. Some have difficulty finishing tasks, even small ones. Many are angry, sometimes directed outward and sometimes turned inward. Feelings of incompetence, lack of spontaneity, avoidance, suspicion, abrasiveness, difficulty handling interruptions, feelings of helplessness and hopelessness… just a few traits of a pastor burning out.

Some become an emotional sponge for everyone's complaints. Some set goals that primarily are intended to prove others wrong. Some eventually define themselves in terms by which their performance and failure in a task becomes failure as a person. Some play it safe to avoid the wrath of a powerful congregant. Some experience conflict in being a leader and a servant at the same time. Some seem as aimless as a blind man's arrow.

Let's check it out: If you are a pastor, take this inventory. Give yourself a 0 (not your problem) to 5 (really your problem) or a score of 2, 3, or 4.

- You are growing increasingly cynical about the value of your ministry.
- You believe you have little effect on how things are going.
- You are growing apathetic about ministry and you hardly care.
- You are starting to act like a robot, doing what you must but only because you must.
- What was once enthusiasm is now turning toward anger and your optimism into despair.
- The casual comments you once brushed off tend to increasingly bother you.
- You are having trouble concentrating on study and sermon preparation.
- You tend to procrastinate more than ever.
- Your trust of others has turned into suspicion and openness into self-protection.

- Your involvement is becoming distant. You tend to withdraw from stress-producing occasions.
- You are more and more impatient with people.
- You have conflicting responsibilities and feel pulled in many directions and you are trying to do everything equally well.
- You have lost much of your sense of humor.
- In the past you never said "no" to anyone, but now out of increasing callousness you are saying "no" to almost everything.
- You are not very confident about the future.
- Your life is highly stressful and you feel helpless to do anything about it.
- You are increasingly absent from the office or study, avoiding people and problems.
- You either overeat or you've lost your appetite.
- You're experiencing some of the physical symptoms of burnout: insomnia, muscular tension, tightness in the chest, rapid heartbeat, rashes, headaches.
- You are increasingly indecisive, irritable, apathetic.
- You normally pride yourself on doing a good job, but you are now looking for short cuts, if not cutting corners altogether.
- You find yourself grieving for past and present losses.
- You are being rewarded (salary, recognition, etc.) less than you deserve.
- You demand much of yourself but more times than not you feel like a failure anyway.

Total_____

If you scored 120, you are totally burned out.
If your score is 0, you are not burned out at all.

If your score is in between somewhere, especially if you are 60 (half) or more, you are closing in on possible burnout. I claim no scientific accuracy for this check up, but believe it is a reasonable tool to help any pastor to begin to understand himself.

How did you fare? Allow me to assume you are near burnout, if not already there and ask: How does a pastor protect himself against the burnout process? Out of my experience let me suggest:

1. Recognize that you may be trying to do too much
Most ministers believe that they are in the most important vocation in the world. This drives pastors to go beyond balance, to command themselves with countless "shoulds," "musts" and "mores," to say "Yes" when they should say "No." Overwork is an offense to the gospel of rest. Diminish intensity, detach, laugh. Remember there are neurotics in the church who may well ask more of you than God does.

2. Realize that you may be at risk of termination
Compassion fatigue is one of the two top conditions putting a pastor at risk of vocational loss. To be burning out or burned out and not realize it or do nothing about it is to risk forced resignation.

3. Establish some realistic goals and long-term priorities
Develop a personal mission statement. What is really important to you? Avoid the tyranny of the present and the urgent by establishing the important. Reassess your goals periodically. Be purpose-driven. "Doors don't slam open," said John Stranahan, creator of *Hooked on Phonics*. Goals are opening doors, determining what is the will of God, looking for opportunities and going straight for them, leaving behind possibilities not fitting with your purposes.

4. Assess your abilities; accept your inabilities

The Bible lists twenty-two spiritual gifts. None of us have all of them. We have God-given abilities and our share of inabilities. Identify your gifts. Face yourself. Get centered in the person God made you to be. Enjoy yourself. Embrace your strengths; look for others to do what you cannot.

5. Recognize that you don't have control over everything

You are not the general manager of the world. You are not indispensable. "The art of being wise is the art of knowing what to overlook," said William James. Hold some things loosely, if at all.

6. Learn to delegate

This is the alternative to saying no. Instead of refusing to be recruited beyond the time available for it or the gifts needed, if it is to be done, empower others; ask them to do what you cannot or should not, allow them freedom, even to fail, celebrate their successes and relax.

7. Reach out for help; make close friends, especially with strong people

Much of your counseling work is with people weakened by the circumstances, depressed by life, failures at least in their own eyes. You need strong friends who restore the grace in you that others devour.

8. Bring the church into the process of recovery

The church must bear some responsibility for the burnout of its pastors, as the next chapter shows. No full recovery happens unless the church's leadership gets involved. Healing begins with honest and open conversation initiated by you. There are scores of people in your congregation who would love to help you prioritize or, if needed, support your recovery.

9. Pace yourself

You can only do so much, and less if you don't balance your work with times of relaxation and pleasure. Question the value of multitasking, if it rules your life. Take the "hectic" out of your life.

10. Take better care of your body

One denomination's study of their pastors (all male) showed that 23 percent were obese and another 34 percent overweight. The Christian Coaching Center reports that 80 percent of pastors do not take a day off and 62 percent sleep only five to six hours a night. Such numbers indicate that pastors would do well to give greater attention to issues of physical health. Walk, play tennis, golf, perspire, routinely sleep eight to nine hours a night, relax. Eat nutritious food. For depression, cardiovascular exercise is very beneficial because it boosts the level of serotonin regulating your mood. Go to the gym to build your tolerance for stress. Be sure to get an annual check up. Taking care of your body is to "love the Lord your God with all your strength" (Mark 12:30).

CONCLUSION

Burnout is a slowly progressing condition, slow as a tortoise taking its time. Early symptoms must be recognized and changes made "while it is yet day." Wherever you are on the spectrum of fatigue and frustration, it may be time to take the possibility of burnout seriously. If you are on the edge of it, get some help now. Unless you don't care to protect your future. Unless you want to live longer under the lone broom bush.

MY STORY—MIKE

"I was forced to resign my church. I still have not recovered. I thought I could just shake it off and continue as usual… but…

"I have a motivational disorder. For every thought to go forward, I have five or six as to why not. Our church grew from 80 to 370 in fifteen months. We built a new sanctuary and filled it. But a group with an agenda starting creating trouble. Did not like losing power. I kept our battle private, followed the constant advice of my district and tried to be redemptive, and to my astonishment the superintendent demanded I resign. Without charges, without anything but success in my background. He said, "They were settled in the area; I was able to move." So two families regained control of the church (I thought we were all a Christian team, to reach the world).

"Two hundred stood on my lawn wanting me to start another church. But the district said they would pull my papers. Loyalty, one of my biggest faults, I turned them down. I still love Jesus. We had pioneered twenty-three different ministries before this. But this somehow became the straw that broke this camel's back. I was informed that I was that 28th minister to be forced to resign (without any charges, sins, or anything wrong), in a twelve-month period in our district.

"I had to write this. Hope you don't mind... I survived a sheep attack but have turned down seven pastoral opportunities since...."

Note: Mike wrote this on the web a while back.

CHAPTER 2

Burnout—Is The Church Responsible At All?

"...honor those leaders who work so hard for you..."
1 Thessalonians 5:12

When a pastor is burned out, it is generally thought that the fault lies with the pastor. He's weak, unreasonable and has perhaps resorted to professing burnout as an excuse to draw back from his workload. He is bored, ineffective, exhausted, cynical and humorless, a condition he has brought on himself or herself. There are flaws in his character and negative changes in his behavior. Besides that, the congregation is being affected by his fatigue. Fix him or let him go and the problem is solved.

Most of what I read on burnout assumes that the individual is the problem and recovery is a matter of that person changing his thinking, life-style and values. Stop Denying, Avoid Isolation, Change your Circumstances, Learn to Face Yourself, Diminish Intensity in your Life. All good ideas for prevention and recovery but all make the assumption that what needs fixing is the individual, not the institution that serves as his workplace. "But our research argues most emphatically otherwise," write Christina Maslach and Michael Leiter. Their study indicates that the problem is not so much the people themselves but the environment in which they work. While their research was into business organizations as the workplace where burnout occurs, it is clearly applicable to the church as the workplace of pastors and their staff. While pastors can be and are culpable, it is in the workplace of pastors that the risk of burnout grows.

The pastor's workplace must address the major dysfunctions that result in burnout, the exhaustion, cynicism, depression, anxiety and ineffectiveness of its pastors. The cost to the church of such fatigue is too great and our love of the church too intense to simply wink at its considerable involvement in this spiraling epidemic.

Can the church afford the cost of its pastors losing motivation for quality ministry? Can it afford growing hostility, despondency, disillusionment, irritability, rudeness and anxiety associated with burnout? Can the church afford an increase in the exhaustion and absenteeism of its staff, the loss of joy among its pastors, valued pastors leaving for another ministry when the church still needs them? Can a church live with the pessimism and cynicism that comes out in sermons, board and committee meetings and even when the pastor is visiting with potential new members? If this isn't too high a price to pay, a loss of income is often a reflection of the loss of quality ministry, attributable to burnout. Pastors don't die from burnout, but the church comes close to it when it does not recognize that burnout is much more than an individual responsibility. It is at least as much the responsibility of his workplace, the church.

"When a pastor suffers from burnout, the whole church suffers," write Gary McIntosh and Robert Edmondson…."A wise church will take steps to help remedy the situation, not just for the pastor's sake, but for the sake of the entire church." Charles C. Manz wrote, "Above all else effective leadership requires compassion." That being true, what happens to the pastor and church when the pastor suffers compassion fatigue? Can a church be strong if its leader must be compassionate to be effective and yet he is exhausted, weary and hardly cares anymore? Is the church courageous enough to begin thinking what correctives to take to curb the burnout rate among its pastors? Hebrews 13:17 instructs the church to so relate to their leaders that "their work will be a joy, not a burden, for that would be of no advantage to you."

"Burnout," Herbert Freudenberger's term, is the common word used for the exhaustion, cynicism and ineffectiveness of this condition. Dr. Archibald Hart uses the term "compassion fatigue" to refer to much the same condition. Hart's term fits the condition as is found in helping professions such as ministry. It emphasizes the compassion, empathy and challenge there is in caring for the wounded, weak and weary as well as the wanderer, the wasted, the wronged and the worried. For the pastor burnout is compassion fatigue.

Maslach and Leiter identify six causes of burnout in the job environment. Protecting your future as a pastor involves leading the church to address these six at-risk factors:

Work overload
Pastors tend to be conscientious. They expect long hours. Keeping up with multiple expectations and demands is a pastor's hope. However, keeping up with the expectations is hopeless. He keeps a dozen balls in the air at one time but feels unappreciated. As a church grows in size, the more people and events call for his time, attention and compassion. He soon discovers that a congregation will ask for as much as a pastor will give. Most pastors, studies show, have difficulty saying "no." Thus it is easy for him to take on too much and soon feel over his head in work. Exhaustion sets in, his emotions are blunted so he cares less than he did at one time. His energy level weakens and he is not as productive as he

once was. Work becomes monotonous. He takes out his frustrations on others in his workplace. He comes in late to his office and leaves early.

Eighty percent of pastors' spouses feel their spouses are overworked. If anyone knows, they do.

A church must be aware of and address the work overload tendency. Additional staff, a contract stating reasonable expectations, study leave and added vacation, a sabbatical, insisting on a day off and protecting that day against intrusion, providing resources that lessen the energy needed and makes the work less time consuming. I was surprised to learn that in the last church I served the office would not give out our home phone number except in a dire emergency. The church did not want me on call twenty-four hours a day. This is an excellent gift, especially for larger churches, to give its pastors.

For its own sake, a church must insist on whatever it takes to create a "no work overload" attitude in the congregation.

Lack of control

No one controls everything. No one argues for unilateral control by anyone. We all know pastors who try. The opposite of a dictator pastor is the pastor who has little, if any, control. He makes few decisions, especially about the use of finances. Problems dare not be addressed unless "everyone is on board." I tried once to privately solve a problem between two families and ended up being called "a little tin god." As a young pastor, trying to act with some authority, I acted as if I was the Almighty. At least one deacon thought that problem was not my business.

Associate pastors feel the lack of control most intensely. They are usually working toward someone else's goals. He doesn't always get to choose what he does. The budget for his work is controlled by someone else. His work is subject to a senior person's assessment. That piece of folk wisdom is right, "No one is so apathetic or resentful as when he or she is working on someone else's goals."

As a greenhorn, my first ministry was to serve as Bible Club director in a Youth for Christ (YFC) program. In addition to working with kids in clubs, I was to lead the singing in the Sunday night, all church, after-church singspirations, we called them. Knowing something about music, I thought I was to choose the latest songs (nothing like today's multiple worship and praise music) and lead every week. I swung my arms to the beat of the music, just as I had been taught, and kept the singing loud and energetic But behind me sat the YFC director. While I led from the pulpit, he led from his chair…. rambunctious, louder and more fast-paced was his style. I had the crowd singing too slowly or too fast, too this or too that. Frankly, I wanted to turn in my songbook and let him take complete control of the music. And I did! You can't live forever with control given then taken away, especially in the very act of being in control, even though you may have abused that trust.

When a pastor begins to feel that he has little effect on how things go, he begins to detach from the decision-making process, feelings of increasing helplessness and hopelessness develop and feelings of benign resignation set in; to use my grandfather's often used fatalistic mantra, a "that's the way it goes" response to life. Powerlessness is a precursor to weariness, anger and despair.

Role expectations need to be made very clear, especially what the role priorities are. Trust must be given unconditionally and the pastor must later earn it. Micromanagement is to be banned and addressed by the church lay leadership when practiced. Policies must be developed as a shared task. How power is shared must be an early discussion between the pastor and lay leaders.

Insufficient reward

Pastors are rewarded by the church in several ways. The most obvious is salary and other material benefits. Others include job security, the possibility of career advancement, recognition, public and otherwise, gratitude expressed on anniversaries and on other such occasions, and simply by helping to make his work productive and more enjoyable.

A salary survey was taken among the evangelical churches of Chicago's western suburbs. To my surprise, my salary was the least of all the churches similar in size. I dared to ask for a raise and was told "we'll pray about it." Perhaps they still are forty years later. I received no additional salary. It was more than the money. Something weakened inside me and while I left there saying the move was God's will, I fully believe God willed it in part because the leaders excused away additional compensation for its pastor with a promise (?) to pray about it. What happens to you when the budget leftovers, if anything, is the financial reward you receive for faithful work?

Marcus Aurelius wrote, "Every man is worth as much as the worth of what he has set his heart upon." The incalculable worth of the Gospel and the church upon which a godly pastor has set his heart should be one major criterion in any discussion of any reward given to its clergy.

Charles is not in the ministry to get rich. He just could not take it anymore that his salary was always the last item in the budget to be considered… and often there was little left.

When he came to me you could tell it was not the money, however. It was more a matter of unfairness and thoughtlessness, he said. He had dared talk about his income to his leaders. They may have had others reasons to want him to resign but this was "perfect," they said. They had watched him buy a new car, even though it was Chevy's less expensive model. Why did he need more money? His wife was working part-time too. They talked to him as if he was one of the "lovers of money" the Bible talks about. It was humiliating, he said. Especially when they said in effect, how could they follow a pastor with this attitude toward money. They suggested he find another place to serve. When he didn't, they saw that he left that place, announcing to the congregation that they weren't free to say why they had asked for the resignation but that the congregation would trust them. He left and that is when he came to me to talk. After about eleven weeks, he accepted a para-church ministry. The salary was even a little less but it wasn't salary he was looking for anyway… it was respect and some feeling he was loved and appreciated.

One pastor was promised a Christmas offering, but when Christmas came no one said another word about it. One pastor asked for a raise and was given $200 a year; nothing would have been better, he said. Another was told that he would receive $100 for a special task he undertook and five years later he is still waiting for it. A pastor came to me brokenhearted because when Pastor's Appreciation Month came, it was not even mentioned in his church, while other pastors in his local ministerial group recited the nice words of appreciation they had received. When he was asked what his church had done, he could say nothing. These are pastors I know who say nothing to their congregants but have come to me wondering whether or not they should quit.

Breakdown of community

Effective ministry, while visualized by one, is carried out by a team of people committed to that ministry. When a person is burned out, he tends to isolate himself, conflict multiplies and anger and bitterness develops among those who believe the tired one is not pulling his weight in the church. A sense of belonging weakens and staff begins to unilaterally do its own thing with a subsequent loss of the greater effectiveness teamwork brings.

The Bible calls the Church the Body of Christ made up of many parts. Each part is indispensable to the whole. God has made it such so "that there should be no division in the body" (1 Cor. 12:12-27). The Church is a community where people work together, suffer together, rejoice together. Attempting to build an effective ministry with some parts of the Body alienated from the task is like trying to erect a building with architects but no engineers, carpenters but no plumbers, stonemasons but no electricians, roofers but no ordinary laborers. It takes multiple people with differing gifts and training… and it is no less true for building the Body of Christ.

A healthy congregation becomes a community as its members engage in mutual ministries in which teams are responsible and active. In a lively church power is shared. Community does not thrive on self-serving, self-help psychobabble sessions or intellectual debates around esoteric issues. A congregation becomes a community when people are accepted for who they are and grace is a way of life, where people feel needed, that they count, where diversity is celebrated, where risk is applauded, where potential is as important as being proficient and people have the freedom to fail.

"When the work's done right, with no fussing or boasting, ordinary people say, 'Oh, WE did it.'" —Lao-Tzu.

At all costs wise lay leaders will take care to grow and maintain a community sense to their church. Burnout happens without it. Rally around and celebrate the pastor God has given you; insist on solving conflicts and promoting unity and mutuality; tolerate no divisiveness, honor "the less honorable," "the unpresentable," "the weaker parts," (1 Cor. 12:22-24). "Make every effort to keep the unity of the Spirit through the bond of peace." (Eph. 4:3). Encourage mutual ministries to begin and grow. Or do you want the sense of community to break down and deadly fatigue to render your pastoral leadership ineffective?

Absence of fairness

Fairness is defined as trust, openness and mutual respect. Pastors want to be trusted to act in the best interest of Christ and the Church. They want honesty and openness in their relationships with lay leadership. They must give and receive the respect of the congregation. When pastors are not trusted and lay leaders look elsewhere for church direction, when secret decisions are made in unofficial, unannounced and closed meetings, when pastors feel manipulated and used, when pastors are not "esteemed for their work's sake," when seldom is the Scripture taken seriously when it says "obey your leaders and submit to their authority" (Heb. 13:12), it is then that pastors "grow weary in well doing" and begin to slowly burn out.

Churches may have come to distrust a former pastor for good reason. The failure of the former pastor easily transfers to the new pastor, if the congregation is not mindful and prayerful regarding this possibility. It is called projection, a term referring to putting on the new pastor characteristics, good or bad, of former pastors. Pastors are handicapped by such unfairness. Trust erodes, openness begins to shut down and mutual respect weakens.

Distribute rewards fairly. When making decisions about staff cuts, should finances call for it, make them with more than finances in mind. Consider the difficulties involved for each person who could be dismissed. Fairness means asking what contemplated changes will do to pastors and staff, not just the benefit to the church's bottom-line.

When fairness is absent with trust, openness and respect lost, then ineffectiveness, cynicism and exhaustion take their place. That is called "burnout."

Conflicting values

A mismatch may occur at this point. Studies have shown that it is a value to new pastors in particular, recently mentored by theological experts, to teach as they have been taught, while the value held by the church is generally putting the church on the map, so to speak.

Church leadership sometimes agrees on the ends to be sought, (terminal values) but the means for reaching such goals are subject to differing values (instrumental values). These show up in the strategies used for reaching those goals. The goal may be to bring people to faith in Christ and the strategy is "all things to all men that by all means we might win some;" however, the values that others hold might call some strategies compromise, deluding separation, cooperating with liberalism or just expedience. A congregation is wise if it knows what the pastor's values are and how they might be expressed in concrete plans for church life.

CONCLUSION

Burnout is a condition for which pastors must take responsibility, but equally so is it attributable to a pastor's workplace. It calls the church to provide for its pastors a balanced workload, choices and control, recognition and reward, a sense of belonging and teamwork, fairness and trust, openness and mutual respect and values held in common and agreed-upon work based on them. Unless a church wants its pastor to forfeit his future and to sit a little longer under a lone broom bush.

Read Tom's story next and you will find traces of burnout with workplace involvement.

"Congregations need to invest in and protect their pastors... when its spiritual leaders are under attack, the ministries by and for parishioners suffer..." —G. Lloyd Rediger

MY STORY—TOM, AS THIS WRITER UNDERSTANDS IT

Tom was a good pastor. He and his associates served a 600+ member church. He had been the church's Senior Pastor for over a dozen years and frankly, from what I have heard, seemed a bit bored (called "Boreout" sometimes) by his ministerial duties. As the church grew, expectations multiplied and he worked many hours to satisfy all of them, the old "bed at the church" syndrome.

In the congregation was Bill Mertz, a long-time deacon, but for the last several years he had not stood for reelection. He apparently had found a new position in the congregation... the nonelected "Uncle Harold" as Lyle Schaller calls him. Many in the elected leadership wanted to know what Uncle Harold thought about important issues on the Board's agenda, prior to its monthly meetings. After all, if there was a budget shortfall at the end of each year, you could count on Bill Mertz to make it up. Bill had a good heart and sometimes counseled Tom too, and it was helpful to have the budget met every year. But Tom felt his leadership compromised.

Most major committees saw themselves as decision- makers, not so much task forces with hands-on responsibilities. It was a bit before churches began to develop action teams, such as Worship teams, Greeter teams, Community Affairs teams and the like. So the interaction of the congregation was highly fellowship (donuts and coffee?) based. A report on the church called it *Koinonitis*.

Tom and his wife began to play more tennis. Fewer hours were spent at the office. He was too tired to attend meetings as often as he did before. His sermons didn't have the same bite as they did at one time. Then she came for counsel.

The study report on the church was rejected by the lay leadership. It was all to justify Tom, whatever he was doing, they said. He felt deeply the gut-stabbing, wrenching unfairness of their conclusion. Important things didn't seem so important anymore. Compassion seemed to become only passion and directed in ways he later thought was impossible for him.

It was Sunday morning when Tom stood before his congregation, a congregation now knowing the Pastor's indiscretion. He read his resignation, walked with his wife down the center aisle and out the door. He was never to be a full-time pastor again.

Yes, some wept, I am told. Others were just stunned. Some settled on a good psychological conclusion by which to explain Tom's action. Soon most blamed Tom for what he had done to the church but they never did really seek the face of God in self-examination and repentance; never saw how they were implicated in any way, never sought counsel as a congregation. They never saw Tom had been overloaded with work, was heading toward burnout and had lost some of his leadership to Uncle Harold. How unfair was their conclusion that nothing had to be done because the report on congregational life was after all, little more than a way to make Tom and his ideas look good. No one thought of how bored Tom had become with fellowship at only a "donut and coffee" level. No one befriended Tom as he wrestled for control over his life again and no one, with a gentle hand on his shoulder, led him back to the altar, called the whole congregation to that altar and then stayed at that altar until not only Tom was cleansed, but the whole congregation and particularly its leadership "found grace in time of need." No one cried out while the church, albeit unknown to most, cursed itself.

Tom was burned out, the congregation was bummed out and the lay leaders bailed out of any complicity in what eventually led to Tom's sin and the church's shock and suffering. No one excuses Tom, the least being Tom himself. He was loved by many in the church. But consider, if you will, how his workplace may very well have been complicit in this story.

CHAPTER 3

Bummed Out But Not Burned Out "But Watch Yourself…"

R uss would not describe himself as burned out. He was tired and slightly angry. In his own words, he had become increasingly "paranoid". At times he had felt abused, like when people made fun of his accent. On occasion he had felt left out of conversations or meetings of which he felt he should have been a part. Some nights he was so exhausted he cancelled meetings claiming to be sick when he was not… and, of course, the lying bothered him. A few weeks ago, for the very first time, he had gone to the pulpit with only a text and nothing else prepared. Two nights before he talked with me, his Board suggested a project for which he had no heart… and he was weary, worried and wanting to quit. This is not his whole story, but what seemed clearly evident was he was not quite burned out but let's call it "bummed out."

Was I ever burned out? I asked myself. Stressed? Yes. Stressed many times in forty plus years of ministry. Wanting to get out of the pastorate? Yes, about every Monday after some nitpicking comment about the sermon on the Sunday before. Depressed, tired, needlessly hopeless at times? All of them. Worried, suspicious, exasperated, sleepless? At times. But not cynical, panicky, out of control or feeling helpless. Others may disagree, but burnout, while knocking at my door once or twice, never broke down the door. Exhausted, but exhaustion never reached burnout.

I asked Faith, my wife, if ever I seemed burned out. She recited some bad decisions I made, some neglect of her and the family, some escapes I took to get away from it all, some very stressful times, but not classic burnout.

If this is true, why? Maybe it's my personality. Easy going, self-analytical, laid-back, not too aggressive. Perhaps because I could read the mood of the church and leave before it got too hot. Naïve, perhaps. Was it that resignation I carried around with me as if it were an amulet to protect me from being hurt? Or perhaps my well-honed power of denial? Or maybe I took my own advice. More about that later. What about you? Bummed out?

What is "bummed out"? It is growing tired of the dailyness of ministry. It is being weary of meetings night after night, even sermons to prepare week after week. You are restless and beginning to think of seeking a new call or finding a ministry other than the pastorate. You are increasingly tired of spending so much of yourself on people with problems and failures. It is a growing procrastination, a waning enthusiasm, a slackening of innovation and initiative, caring but feeling that very few care for you. It is being battle-weary. The future seems tenuous at best. Or it may be a feeling that ministry has changed so much that you no longer fit with the expectations, particularly of younger church members. Your spouse is stressed and more and more unhappy. It may be sneaky feelings that several in the congregation are ready to have you move. Generally, it is wondering: What difference am I making here anyway? Bummed out is basically a light burnout.

I suspect that the "bummed out" mood I describe is part of the hurried life of most people in ministry at one time or another. Chilled out but not burned out. Not overworked, sufficiently in control, adequately rewarded, treated fairly most of the time, sharing the ministry with eager, gifted congregants, values compatible with the congregation. Bewildered on occasion but not burned out. Worn down but not worn out. Hurt but generally healthy. Weary but not dreary. Frankly, my experience with at-risk and exited pastors has been more with pastors bummed out than burned out. They sit under the lone broom bush, but unlike Elijah, they are still awake. Lie there for a while longer and you are at risk.

A Christian college dean was tired of the scores of pastors who came to him looking for a job. His comment to one (possibly on a bad day) was his feeling about most of them: "Guys like you are a dime a dozen," he said. He wasn't angry, just surprised and later exhausted by too many bummed-out pastors looking to find an honorable way out of pastoral ministry.

- Has much of the joy gone out of sermon preparation for you?
- Do you put things off more frequently than you once did?
- Do people with little problems taking up your time irritate you?
- Do you often think about a non-church ministry or at least another church?
- Have you wondered what difference are you making anyway?
- Does it seem to you that there are a few, maybe quite a few people in the congregation who would be glad for you to move?
- Is your spouse increasingly unhappy with being in ministry? Ask her!

Answers to questions like these will give you a hint, if not a shout, that you are bummed out. If so, you are going to make some decision not good for you or the church. You are going to exhibit some inappropriate anger. You will have debilitating periods of depression. You are going to be grouchy at home. You might still enjoy initiating some things but your poor follow-up will kill what you start. Mail will go unanswered. Even your immunity to disease is compromised. And if you are not careful, someone is going to charm you into her arms. Consequences to being bummed out happen.

Let's talk about what keeps you from being "weary in well-doing" and protects your future against eventual burnout. Here's the talk I've given myself:

1. Setting boundaries

Without boundaries for the use of your time and the workload you will take on, you will at first be well liked for your unlimited availability. Unlike Jesus, you never "come apart for awhile and rest" nor do you ever walk away from a crowd while they ask for more. You said your family comes first (all pastoral candidates say that), but when you don't say "no" though you should, when you try to please everyone, when you think you must prove yourself a hard worker, the fact is your family has come not first, not even second, but third after you and the church. It works while you are a learner but when a few months later you become a leader, your energy for effective leadership has been weakened by your "all things to all people" attempts.

Write down a few boundaries. Time boundaries, work boundaries, relationship boundaries, boundaries of thought and deed, boundaries as to your practice of the spiritual disciplines, physical health boundaries, role boundaries, office/home boundaries, other boundaries appropriate to where God has called you to serve. You will cross them a time or two, so never expect perfection. Here are a few to consider:

- No Saturday night meetings, parties or church chicken dinners.
- No phone calls or counseling sessions in the mornings after 9:00 or 10:00 a.m. (study only).
- Two nights out (preferably one) a week and no more.
- Structured exercise three to four times a week.

- Personal Bible study and prayer daily unrelated to Sunday's sermon.
- Confession before sleep.
- Window in your office door… or keep it open a little.
- Healthy relationships with the opposite sex.
- No fantasizing, daydreaming or putting yourself in the way of temptation.
- Keep the office and home separate.
- Play once in a while, but not playtime for ministry's sake.
- Schedule home time, spouse date time, timeouts and write them in your date book.

Reflect on how you are doing staying behind the boundaries. (To remember, connect your time for self-examination with some regular event in your church. Say, every time you baptize someone.)

Writing this has been a bit painful for me. I've put up many of these fences but I can't go on until I confess to you that I've climbed over, under and around them more times than I want to admit. It's spiritual warfare and I have lost too many battles. By the grace and power of God, you will do better.

2. Being accountable

A pastor-friend asked me: "What has God said to you today?" I got flushed and a little mad. Who was he that I should give account to him? The answer was "nothing" and that's why I resented being asked that question. I had skipped time alone with God that day.

I had breakfast with Bill Hybels, the Willow Creek Church Pastor. He asked that I offer thanks. I did. "There is something wrong with your spiritual life. I can tell by your prayer," he said. I was surprised and a little ticked but Bill was right. No one had ever said that to me before. Senior Pastor, Vice-President of his college, preacher to thousands on occasion, and a big enough man for this busy super-pastor not to refuse breakfast with me. And he calls me to account for my spiritual laxness.

For forty years I had a friend with whom I confided most every struggle, failure or success. Years ago he was diagnosed with Alzheimer's Disease and now he doesn't even remember me. So there goes a longtime confidant, a friend to whom I was accountable.

Accountability is another tough discipline for me. Recently, I took the PRO-D personal survey. It was very helpful and extremely positive. One caution area, however, got right to the point: "Tend to take things personally." That's why accountability is hard for me and perhaps for you.

Accountability relationships, at their best, provide encouragement, perspective, guidance, feedback, affirmation, linking with needed resources, and possibly intervention when needed. It's more than confession and the assurance of forgiveness. It's more than uncovering what you must no longer hide. It is more than revealing dark secrets. It is more than friendship.

A good accountability relationship has in it trust, confidentiality, honesty, accessibility, grace, humility, perseverance, protection, prayer and unhurried time.

I hate accountability. I need accountability. If I wait until I love it, I'll never seek such a bond. It takes time to grow a relationship so today is the day to begin. A seminary friend? A support group? A trustworthy elder? Someone vulnerable himself but nonetheless candid. Never your spouse.

Proverbs 27:17 says, "As iron sharpens iron, so one man sharpens another." Who sharpens you?

3. Connect with and care for yourself

Driven people, busy people, overly engaged people often have eyes for everyone else's needs but too little care for themselves. It feels like self-centeredness, if not selfishness, when it is essentially self-care. You must make time for yourself. Stop trying to be a "bionic" minister. Relax and appreciate the day you are living. If you make a mistake, never think of yourself as a mistake. Never think you are bad because you have thought about leaving the ministry. Share people-helping responsibilities, rather than doing everything yourself. Bolster your life with regular times of prayer and meditation unrelated to your work. Structure a sabbatical into your support arrangements with the church. See your physician regularly. Don't expect to keep everybody happy—there are neurotics in every church. Avoid the lure of easy pleasure by which you bankrupt your spirit.

Accept yourself for who you are. If you want to burn out, try to be someone else. Wish every day for the tools some other pastor has. Accept that whatever may be your limitations, they are not obstacles to ministry but indications of where God wants to take you in ministry. Accept where you are strong. It is not humility to put yourself down; it is pretense, better yet, nonsense. Acknowledge the gifts God has given you. You didn't merit or acquire them on your own, so recognize them, accept them, celebrate them. Others need you to be what God made you to be. Connect with yourself and accept yourself... or try being someone else and your failure will be a huge step to being bummed out.

4. Cast away weighty worries

Worry disarms your soul leaving you half-paralyzed and unable to maintain equilibrium, think objectively and pray confidently. It crowds the mind leaving you unable to consider solutions. It is as futile as a rain dance in Death Valley.

So you didn't make a good impression when you wanted to; yes, you were overlooked; you live with some regret about the past; you lied to save your skin and its possible disclosure haunts you; you said "no" to someone who doesn't seem to forget it; you saw a little meeting going on and you're sure you were the agenda; you got angry at an elders' meeting; you've got mysterious and maybe mortal pains; where will the money come from to educate your children. There are many more crippling and preventing you from living to the fullest. You can always find something to worry about.

It is rotten fruit making you sick. It is a false prophet offering deadly advice. It is a promethean vulture eating away at your life. It is cancer and who among us would let cancer go untreated? Rightful action is time well invested; worry is time irretrievably spent.

Worries when coddled fester and spread. But it's not the problems that hurt us; it is the way we treat the problems. There is nothing to do with them but to let them go (a hundred times a week, if necessary) and to "cast your anxiety upon him, because he cares for you" (1 Pet. 5:7). Live the moment, not the past or future. Get some help, if need be. Someone said "Don't let your worries get the best of you; remember, Moses started out as a basket case."

5. Nurture and enlarge the joy in your life

Why do I suggest this affirmation? Here's the answer: "…the joy of the Lord shall be your strength" (Neh. 8:10). Someone has said that joy is the feeling of grinning on the inside. It is that and more. Strength is joy's overflow. Joy is stuffed with strength. The nerve and muscle of the power to stand when others fall is joy. Not pleasure for pleasure is incompatible with pain. Joy is strength transcending pain (2 Cor. 7:4b). Joy gives the soul stoutness and stability. When joy is absent or weak, we are vulnerable to temptation. "Joy unspeakable and full of glory" is the guardian of the heart when otherwise circumstances would break it. Joy slays the bummed-out feeling.

You ask: How is joy nurtured and enlarged?
By living in the presence of God. Psalm 16:11
By meditating in the Word of God. Psalm 19:8; Jeremiah 15:16; John 15:11

By worshipping God. Psalm 71:23
By humbling before God. Isaiah 29:19
By pleasing God. Ecclesiastes 2:26
By asking and receiving from God. John 16:24
By trusting in God. Romans 15:13

Ultimately, joy is a lively relationship with God. Psalm 43:4 refers to God as "my joy and my delight." God is joy and to be intimate with Him is intimate joy. A close relationship with God is indispensable (Ps. 21:6). As Michael Quoist puts it, "The measure of your intimacy with God is precisely the measure of your joy." Intimacy with God = joy = strength = not bummed out or burned out. But remember, while joy is freely given it is not freely received. To receive it is as costly as steadily maintaining a lively relationship with God ... which brings me to my final point.

6. Remember again who God is

Of great value in every situation is to know intimately what the attributes, character and presence of God means to that situation. Can change happen? God is omnipotent. Am I really alone? God is omnipresent. Do I have access to the wisdom I need in this situation? God is omniscient. Grace when "nothing in my hand I bring; simply to thy cross I cling"; love, when I feel unloved and unlovely; mercy when the pain is too much.

I read of a five-year-old boy so rambunctious that his parents feared he might hurt his baby brother. So when they heard their precocious son talking to his little brother, they opened the baby's bedroom door to listen. To his month old sibling, newly from heaven he thought, he was saying, "Tell me what God is like. I am forgetting." Perhaps your situation with the church seems abusive, or at the least you feel betrayed and bewildered. Are you forgetting what God is like?

CONCLUSION

You may not be burned out. You need not be. If Alban Institute is right, 17 percent of pastors are burned out at any one time, which means 83 percent are not. Congratulations for being on the good side of the statistics. But don't discount the possibility of "a lone broom bush" in your future unless you take steps to protect your future and restore yourself, if indeed you are bummed out.

MY STORY—HARRY

This is my story. I was graduated from seminary in 1989 and went to my first church within three months of getting out of school. I was married and in two years we had a little boy we named Ricky. He wasn't in the best of health from the very beginning.

The church was small but we enjoyed it. Leaving there for a church twice as large four years later was a step up but in some ways a step down. The church had pushed its last pastor out and they thought I could heal all the problems and get the church back on the road again. I worked at it; day and night I worked at it. But I didn't get too far and the Board let me know they were a little disappointed. I became the problem. So I worked harder. Went to meetings galore. Tried to visit people when they were sick, solve a division between a brother and sister with no success, took no vacation for the next two years, but after a while I just wanted to give up. Most people thought my preaching was good, but you know how it is, a few people complaining is all you can think about. I began to wonder if it was doing any good. They complained by their pocketbooks. I wondered whether or not I should look around and find another church but frankly, I was beginning to get down on the church, period. I was exhausted, I guess. People were so petty. I tried to avoid them but how could I? One winter I got so sick that I hardly felt like doing anything.

I told the Board I was tired and needed time off. At the time I told them, we had three people in the hospital, one of them an old-time board member. So they said they would talk about it later. I would go to the hospital to visit, go to Board meetings like any good pastor would but it felt like going through the motions, that's all. I was just tired of daily ministry.

Then Ricky got really sick. He lived about four months, I guess, and nothing seemed to work with him. I've never had such pain in all my life… my wife began to get bitter at God and I could hardly blame her.

I began to think, and I still do, that I was just a failure at being a pastor. I just couldn't keep living the way we had to live, so Marian and I decided we would take some time for ourselves and I resigned after more than eight years in that place, a place that nearly killed me and almost destroyed our marriage.

After I resigned, I was told that if I hadn't quit, several people would have asked the Board to ask me to move on.

We expected to be out for a couple of years but it has been six years now and I sometimes want to get back and sometimes I don't. I think about whether or not I was even called to be a pastor. I'm working but don't have meetings every night and thoughtless people to deal with and although we stayed away from church for a while we now go most every Sunday, but that's it. It took the life out of me and I haven't really recovered yet, so why should we ever go back? Right or wrong, that's the sad story.

I never heard anyone in seminary tell me that churches could be so hard on their pastors… so unempathetic to a pastor's pain. The first time I was asked to tell my story was… you guessed it… when Chuck asked me to write this piece.

I should say too that we have had two healthy children since Ricky's death.

CHAPTER 4

Vision Conflict:
Onward, Christian Soldiers,
Marching As To War
(You Betcha!)

"Blessed are the peacemakers…"
Matthew 5:9

Ten studies over a dozen years and all but one came to the same conclusion. I created the survey and Jay Spencer, a PhD student, validated it by using it with more than 250 pastors of his denomination. The conclusion: the primary stressor experienced by pastors, leading most often to forced resignation, is VISION CONFLICT, the ugly pastor/pew rift over how the life and work of a particular church is to be understood and acted upon. It is primary in the terrible phenomena of pastors at risk and forced resignations.

Dr. Samuel Blizzard, a pioneer in the exited pastor phenomenon, found decades ago that the major reason pastors left vocational ministry then was the realization that God could be served in any honorable profession. Not so today. Survey after survey and the personal testimony of hundreds of pastors show that the primary reason for pastors leaving ministry today (and hyper-stressed while in it) is vision conflict. Vision is crucial to the church but vision conflict is so prevalent as to seem almost inevitable.

Pastor and parishioner agree with Scripture that without vision, people are unrestrained (Prov. 29:18). Without a vision they tend to go in every direction without boundaries. Most everyone would agree also with Dr. Norman Shawchuck, "A congregation is at its best when vision is breaking out all over." When visions are breaking out all over, however, the congregation may be at its worse. If "visions" are multiple and opposed to each other, that church is "marching as to war." It's vision conflict, a pastor's number one affliction.

First, what is vision? Jonathan Swift wrote, "Vision is the art of seeing the invisible." Warren Bennis said, "Vision is a working dream." Norman Shawchuck observed, "Vision is God's dream dreamed in us." Terry Fullam defines vision as "the product of God working in us. God creates the vision and we receive it." As such it is an epiphany coming to us from beyond us and larger than we could dream or plan. While it is projected onto the screen of the church, it is planted in us by the Spirit of God alive in us. It is God's desired future for us, the intoxication of the Holy Spirit.

Vision is not a mere wish, a condition we hope for but never expect to happen. It has often been called a dream, but it is not simply a dream that gets into our emotions and is generally too good to be true. We have a wish or a dream, but a vision has us, shaping us more than shaping our future.

Vision, however, is more than hopeful, passionate desires. It is not contained in academic definition alone. It is tears, sleepless nights, prayers without answers. It often has depression as its strange bedfellow, fear as its unwanted companion and impatience trying to drag it to a premature death. Vision cannot be compared with a ship on calm seas, a painting in pastels, a day of clear skies and balmy winds. It's not simply a good idea, a meritorious wish or somebody's viewpoint. It is a word from God, held deeply in one's spirit and life-changing in its possibilities.

The need for vision in a congregation cannot be overemphasized. It is extremely costly when a congregation is in conflict. When people have a vision, it lifts the congregation to new realizations of its possibilities. It brings clarity where there is obscurity, generates power and enthusiasm, aligns thoughts, emotions and actions and breathes life into what otherwise is threatening to become a corpse. It restructures relationships, redistributes resources and renews communication.

Now to the issue of vision conflict and its resolution.

G. Douglas Lewis wrote, "I define conflict as two or more objects trying to occupy the same space." Lay leadership on the one side, and the pastor and/or staff on the other trying "to occupy the same space" with differing insights, values and ideas. Actual or perceived differences regarding needs, interests, actions, facts, methodology, authority and responsibility turn into conflict. At the root is communication failure and often simply personality differences. Conflict at times occurs over role definitions, pastoral expectations, theological differences, worship styles and music in particular, social issues, leadership, purpose, programs and property.

Before considering the management of vision conflict or harnessing it and directing it, you should know:

- Conflict is not *a priori* sinful. Sin is conflictual but conflict by itself is not.
- Leaving conflict unmanaged is a sin of omission.
- It is costly to resolve conflict, but more costly not to do so.

- If conflict over vision is not resolved, the success of the vision accepted will be short-lived.
- Resolving conflict is much more than preventing a fight.
- Confrontation may be necessary, but never separation.
- Each side in a conflict has truth in it.
- The best way to resolve conflicts is to deal with them before they start.
- Discovering God's mind can mean deliberately engaging in conflict. (Matt. 21; John 8). When you believe that out of problems can come new life, maturity and growth, then conflict can lead to a richer, more creative ministry, when handled properly.
- Corporate and creative prayer plays a major role in transforming and managing conflict.
- Every pastor should have conflict management training. Check the Internet for options. At least, read a book on the topic.

With these concepts as presuppositions to how we see vision conflict, consider these ideas (by no means is this a mini- course in conflict resolution).

1. **God gives vision to people, not committees**, though a committee may confirm it. Abraham had a vision, as did Samuel, David, Ezekiel, Daniel, Zechariah, Paul, Peter and others. If God gives a vision to a pastor, an epiphany, it is not unusual that the pastor alone receive it, to be confirmed by others. This does not exclude others involved in developing the vision, but precedent indicates that the pastor receives and casts the vision, arousing the church with it and taking the lead in fulfilling what it requires. The church, hoping to avoid vision conflict, will affirm this process as right and good.

2. **Conflict is an expected state for church life.** Conflict is inevitable and a part of what business calls the "form, storm, norm and perform" process of developing an idea. Carlyle Marney said it well, "The church in tension is the church in its natural habitat." Newton Maloney said, "Conflict has been the essence of the way the church has purified itself from within through the years." Archibald Hart believes that "40 percent of pastors say they have a serious conflict with a parishioner at least once a month." Can it be more normal to the church than that indicates?

Seventy-nine of the 149 clergy who responded to Barbara Gibson's questionnaire (53 percent) indicated that at some time during their ministry they had experienced major conflict with parishioners or staff. To be forewarned is to be forearmed.

3. **Vision casting is a primary role of the senior pastor.** Carl George of the Fuller Evangelistic Association may have been first to say this. A church will avoid much conflict if its leadership confirms this as true, that this is the role of the senior pastor. It must be caught by the pastor first, of course, and developed with the involvement of the leadership and other congregants and then it can be cast. But vision casting is the pastor's task. Affirming this may well prevent some conflict.

4. **Conflict in vision is often over things not worth the time and energy we give it.** Dean Hoge wrote, "Congregations clash over small things." Pastors have told me of churches clashing over the color of the carpet, custodial duties and salaries, Sunday worship times in the summer, contemporary music and whether or not to use choir robes.

5. **In conflict there is enough blame to go around.** "Quarrels would not last long if the fault was only on one side," said La Rochefoucauld. Vision may be divinely given but it is humanly received. It mixes with temperament, ego, or sometimes with a desire for a certain way so that "you may spend what you get on your pleasures" (James 4:3).

6. **Denying it, stuffing it and endlessly delaying it will never solve vision conflict.** You've got to start talking about it. Communication solves conflicts. Silence exacerbates them. Talk! If only for ten minutes; then twenty and before long talk more. Start where it is safe and where there is agreement (probably your values or with your own contributions to the conflict). Clearly identify and define the problem of conflict as a problem for all the congregation. Clarify, note differences and identify sources. Talk about it openly and honestly. Brainstorm solutions.

7. **In conflict know when to quit.** Have you heard of the "law of holes"? It is simple: if you are in a hole, stop digging. When pastoring in oil-field country, I heard roustabouts say to their preachers (including me), "If you don't hit oil in twenty minutes, quit drilling." A strategic stop can be worth more than a stubborn go. When your discussion emotionally escalates, schedule your next meeting and say the benediction. When a satisfactory conclusion is reached, albeit not perfect, stop then, too. At the least agree to disagree, for the time being, and go on with your life.

8. **Listen, listen, listen**. Not just hear, waiting for your turn to speak; listen. Be slow to speak. No interruptions. Understand the other's point of view. Say what you hear back to your opponent in your own words. Restate it until you understand it. Value what everyone says. Encourage quiet members to speak. Listen for

assumptions and clarify them. Listen for emotions and respond to them ("I hear you saying you love this church."). Be sure to listen even if what is said is an exaggeration, a generalization, inconsistent or unreasonable. "All wise men share one thing in common: the ability to listen," said Frank Tyger.

9. **Conflict wilts when its participants seek resolution governed by love.** Love is not the opposite of conflict, but of hate. I mean agape, the love described in 1 Corinthians 13 as unconditional and sacrificial. Not some amorphous itching around your heart you can't scratch. Be patient, kind, not envious, boastful or proud. Love is not rude, self-seeking, easily angered and doesn't keep records of wrong done or said. Does not delight in evil. Rejoices with the truth. Protects, trusts, hopes, perseveres, never fails. Two or more conflicting visions find resolution when this quality of love is embraced and practiced, even imperfectly. Just think what patience, kindness and trust alone would do, when conflict occurs. Remember, "Fear knocked on the door; love answered, and no one was there."

10. **"In those who disagree, look for the positive, the true, noble, right, pure, lovely, admirable, excellent or praiseworthy." (Phil. 4:8)** In conflict it is natural to look for weaknesses; instead, look for strengths. In opposition we look for error; look for the right and true. In arguments we wish for the others' failure; encourage success. In controversy, our pride is at stake; humble yourself. We desire to teach; be teachable (meekness). We delight in a win/loss; pray for a win-win result. In conflict our motives may be questionable; be sure they are pure. In arguments, we generally begin with where we disagree; look for where you agree. To win we hold grudges; forgive. In conflict, we are tempted to threaten, punish, shame or lay guilt on each other; how "lovely" is that? Think about someone opposed

to your vision. Identify something good about him/her, or something good another said about him/her. Go to that person and say, "You know what I admire about you?" Then genuinely express what you admire in him/her. See what that does to your relationship. Max Lucado said, "Conflict is inevitable, but combat is optional." Combat becomes unthinkable when Philippians 4:8 thinking rules.

11. **When confrontation is necessary, confront according to Scripture** such as found in Matthew 18:15-20. Private confrontation comes first. Reconciliation is the goal. Humility and mercy are to govern the conversation. Be gentle, forgiving, confidential, assessing your own possible contribution to the conflict.

12. **Set appropriate boundaries**. Begin your discussions by setting boundaries for the process, conversation, etc. Discuss only one sentence of a potential vision statement at a time. You will talk all together, not in self-appointed groups. You will stick to the subject. You will not get personal. Attack the problem, not the person. You will brainstorm solutions with all alternatives received with thought and grace.

13. **Call in a Christian mediator, if necessary.** Ask for help. A mediator won't necessarily solve the conflict but will guide the process toward resolution, urging biblical faith and practice.

14. **Draw up a covenant at the end of a successful resolution, even though it might not be total.** Include how the solution will be carried out. Then celebrate! Covenant to live together as members of the same Body, the Body of Christ, humbled by the process, committed to prayer for the future, not giving bad reports about those with whom you were in conflict (James 4:11-12).

CONCLUSION

Vision conflict is a primary stressor for congregations and pastors. Churches are divided; pastors lose their positions. God is dishonored. The watching world laughs. If you cannot resolve it, then harness and direct it. Make it work for the good of the church. Don't let it just slide. Managing conflict in a timely way will protect the future for a pastor at risk as well as be a guard against present loss.

MY STORY—REVEREND MARK

I had wanted to be a preacher like my grandfather even at the tender age of six, so when I graduated from the seminary in 1985, I began to live my dream of telling people about Jesus.

After serving for three years in a 120-year congregation in my denomination, I received a call to be a church planter in a small town of 500. I planted a church and was pastor there for eight years, and God grew that church to about 725 members. Life was large and ministry was successful. Then in 1996 at thirty-seven years old, I received a call to become the senior pastor of a large congregation in the suburbs. I felt as though I was moving up the church ladder to bigger and better things.

I accepted that call and from day one was met with opposition when I was told by newly elected congregational leaders that they were not in those positions to help me but to keep me in my place. Every step I took was closely watched and scrutinized. Though the small group of dissidents kept their attacks coming, the church grew from an average worship of 450 to almost 1000 in ten months.

During my time at this church I would find my pager, voice mail, and mailbox filled with messages of discouragement and hatred. Notes of things not done and that I was supposed to do were taped to my office door and slid under the door. My young children were confronted by angry adults with words like, "Tell your father to get the hell out of here; we don't want him here." As the tension mounted, my spirit was dying.

My days were long, my spiritual life dry, my family barely knew me. After only ten months, in April of 1997, I found myself sitting in an Elders meeting being accused of things beyond my wildest imagination. I was confronted with the question I had been asked many times before, "If you don't want to live by the rules and regulations of our beloved synod, why don't you just leave?" In brokenness and with no fight left in me, I took the offer, giving my resignation on the spot.

My life dream was seemingly shattered. Everything I had hoped to do and be, were apparently gone. Who was I? What would I do? I love the "Church"; why couldn't it love me? I was convinced I was the problem and felt I was the only pastor to ever be forced out of ministry.

About a year later I found the ministry of Pastor-in- Residence. Because of their work, I know who I am and once again am doing what I was called to do.

CHAPTER 5

Can We Talk?
Isolation And Loneliness

"The Lord God said, 'it is not good for the man to be alone...'" One stress upon a pastor's spouse is that she has no pastor. Come to think of it, one stress of a pastor himself is no pastor. To use Barbara Gibson's phrase, a pastor is often "all stressed up and nowhere to blow."

Perhaps a problem of the pastor's own doing, he is isolated and lonely. He needs an understanding ear to listen to him when he needs to talk. Often he enlists few if any genuine friends who unconditionally support him, especially when he is open and transparent about the good and the bad of his life.

When the pastor chooses to talk to his judicatory people, he jeopardizes his career; when he opens up to other pastors, competition multiplies; when he befriends a member of the congregation, he is thought to be partial; when he talks with extended family, they won't believe he feels so alone. He preaches "if we walk in the light..." but he feels his position demands a certain professional, perhaps benign, salutary hiding... and that is isolating and lonely.

A deadly condition

Isolation and loneliness, according to Wikipedia, is "a powerful surge of emptiness and solitude." It is feelings of isolation even in a crowd, thus different from aloneness. It is a feeling of seclusion and separateness. It is sometimes accompanied by feelings of abandonment, rejection and insecurity. Feeling that no one understands or has any compassion for his plight, the lonely person, almost in schizophrenic fashion, pushes himself into conversation with himself and finds growing paranoia and depression. Longing for company but finding it difficult to make contact with others, he has only one friend, himself.

Wikipedia startled me with this statement: "Chronic loneliness… is a serious life-threatening condition. At least one study has empirically correlated it with an increased risk of cancer, especially those who hide their loneliness from the outside world" (Quoted in Wikipedia article on Loneliness by Eleanor Smith. *Psychology Today*, Article 7. May 1988). A study by Dr. James S. House shows social isolation compares with cigarette smoking and other major medical conditions as a physiological risk factor (*Psychosomatic Medicine* 63, 2001, p. 373).

Neuroscientist John T. Cacioppo observes that lonely people have greater resistance to blood flow leading to high blood pressure. They produce more stress hormones which is "like they're always revving their engines in the red resulting in impaired immunity, less restful sleep, cardiac problems and a tendency to be more hostile. They eat foods with higher contents of sugar and fat, which tends toward obesity and that can be devastating. It hurts right down to the cellular level."

One study suggests that social rejection literally makes you feel cold… the cold shoulder idea. In a 2006 article in *USA Today* (dated April 23, 2006) the author (staff writer) remarks, "Loneliness really might break your heart." Social skills tend to atrophy through misuse and disuse. Less exercise is common and daytime fatigue increases. It speeds up aging. It negatively affects learning and memory. It's a killer.

When lonely, we tend to withdraw into our work, possessions and pastimes (golf, tennis, hobbies). Sometimes lonely people withdraw into fantasies and daydreams. Physically and psychologically, loneliness hurts.

Isolation and loneliness are no mere misfortune without consequence. Yet a majority of pastors report they feel isolated and lonely, without significant recourse to others, even though in the presence of a crowd. The need is for communion, connection and conversation, all three present and interacting as one.

Realizing that loneliness is not healthful, the answer is not simply getting friends, a cat and a spouse, jerking yourself out of the slough of isolation, and living happily ever after. What can pastors do about loneliness?

First, I wish to remind you of a biblical truth that impacts this discussion.

An established connection

Any discussion of loneliness for the Christian must include a rehearsal of what connections have already been established between people of the faith. Feelings of loneliness are mitigated in part by recognizing that we are connected with thousands of people in the Body of Christ, of which we are a part. Romans 12 makes it clear that we are, whether we realize it or not, members of the same Body, "each one of you is part of it" (v. 27). We are in fellowship with each other. Connectiveness is established at its root and that gives us the freedom and privilege to pursue it experientially. You *are* in fellowship; now *be* in fellowship is the thrust of Romans 12's description of how the Body is to operate. While not alone, we need not be lonely.

A support group

Many treatments for chronic loneliness have been offered. It is not my intention to recite these. For pastors, one absolute necessity looms large: pastors must have support groups to which they belong.

Sixty-six percent of all pastors have no support group. Another study says 70 percent. One personal study set the number at 75 percent. Pastors usually are reluctant to talk about themselves. Some people think of a pastor as someone more than human, and many of us buy into the false image. Fear of losing face, grace and place keeps pastors to themselves. Vulnerability is too high a risk. As is transparency. "No One Understands Like Jesus," so it is safe to talk with Him, but "No One" else understands, so we think. Some pastors say they are too busy or self-sufficiency is godliness to others. In the meantime, isolation and loneliness continue as silent clergy-killers.

A pastor's support group is often a group of one, the pastor's spouse. How destructive to a marriage can that be? According to Shiloh.com, half of all clergy marriages end in divorce. If a pastor brings all the stresses of ministry home at night and the day off is conversation about church problems and members who "think otherwise," is the clergy divorce rate really a surprise?

What is a support group? It is a small group, preferably of pastors, who regularly meet for conversation and connection, some measure of accountability and fellowship, with limited structure. It is best when several denominations are represented, where its members are vulnerable and candid with each other, where non-judgmental attitudes and differences are normal and all are accepted in God's grace.

It is not difficult:

- Take the lead and establish a support group, perhaps with just a couple others.
- On the first meeting, take the lead in being transparent, vulnerable and candid.
- Together agree on its purpose and expectations.

- Decide where and how often you will meet.
- Determine manner of accountability. Perhaps decide this later when you have met awhile.
- Make clear the level of confidentiality.
- Consider other interactions in addition to meeting.
- Evaluate after about a year.

Isolation is not healthy, relationally, psychologically and physiologically. Being an introvert is no excuse. Busy, yes, but every pastor is busy. Breaking out of isolation is not your priority. Temperamentally you are phlegmatic. So you continue to destroy the temple of the Spirit. Why not find a friend in ministry this week and simply say, "Can we talk?"

Isolation and loneliness, even with others all around, are much too common. It is a killer. It puts you at risk and, sad to say, many do not realize it until they have gone from at risk to exodus.

MY STORY—JASON, AS TOLD BY BRANDAN

We went through seminary together, then combat. We were chaplains serving in Vietnam. He was Jason and I am Brandan (called Bran by my friends). He can't tell his story but I will try to give you a feel for what it was like and how overwhelming ministry became for Jason.

One morning in Vietnam was unforgettable for us. A firefight with the Viet Cong had been devastating to two companies of the 173rd Airborne Brigade. We were there listening to gunfire in the distance, helicopter gunship rotors whirling and, most devastating, the groans of wounded and dying soldiers.

To those wounded and alive we spoke of Christian hope for a moment or two, then loaded them in a waiting rescue-equipped Huey. Later we helped move the dead to the edge of the tarmac for transport back to base. The story was to repeat itself again and again with equal anguish and distress for us, until it came time (finally) to muster out. You never forget times like these.

We both took churches in Memphis, Tennessee. They both grew rapidly. Then something seemed to happen to Jason. He lost his sense of humor and lightness. He shared some of his burdens with me for a while but increasingly he found it difficult to talk about the frustrations he was feeling.

After playing volleyball together one Thursday, I tried to help him with "Jason, the Lord never intended that we bear our burdens alone. We can pray for you and help wherever we can. Please let us…"

With a look of sadness on his face, he spoke: "Are you kidding, Bran? Ministers are not supposed to have problems. If we talked about them, we can kiss our career good-bye. Even our own people don't really understand."

After Sunday night service, Jason was tired and troubled, his wife told me. He wrote a short note to his family, then placed a .357 Magnum revolver in his mouth, pulled the trigger and Jason was gone. My friend was gone!

My wife and I rushed to Jason's house when we heard and with his wife faced an awful grief and loss.

You probably find it hard to understand a minister committing suicide. But a minister can become desperate too, yet he dare not let others know his fears and frustrations because he will not be really understood. Often he will be viewed as a loser by fellow ministers, his congregation, his denomination, sometimes even by his family.

To whom does a pastor go to talk openly about his needs, his problems, and his fears? His battles? Do fellow pastors or his denomination care? Yes, they do. But their pressures are large too… and time is not always available. So it happens and it happened to my friend.

Note: Jason exited ministry—by his own hand. But couldn't others of us and our churches have helped in any way? Could we understand that our pastors are human too? I ask you.

MY STORY—JOHN

My name is John. I have been serving the Lord for most of my life. After many years of running, I had to confront a growing problem in my life. I could not control my personal finances. It soon became an all-consuming downward spiral. The fear of exposure caused me to continually try to work harder. Even though I did not consider myself a workaholic, I was driven to avoid my real problem, no matter what it took.

Eventually, I received a new appointment to a church in a new state and believed sincerely that I could start fresh. Unfortunately, I was wrong. The ministry there went well, but my financial situation became so desperate that I could no longer hide. The results were devastating to everyone around me.

It was at that time that I was introduced to Pastor-in- Residence. I began to realize I could face my problems and know that fellow believers would be there to walk with me and hold me accountable. I at last had people with whom I could be honest and they would hear me.

In looking back, I realize that it was very difficult for me to be real with the men serving alongside me, especially the Senior Pastor. You may not agree but many times it seems that a failure of a staff member is really failure on his part as well. I realize, though, that this is not an easy challenge to overcome. Many times I wanted to talk to other staffers, but did not feel that I could trust them or that they then would trust me. I'm sure that my emotions clouded my judgment about this, but it seemed very real to me at the time. I felt I had no one to talk to. I had to carry my burden alone.

I don't want this to sound as if I am blaming others for my problems; I just know that early on there was no mechanism in place for me to be able to talk about my problems with the people closest to me in the ministry. I had nowhere to go so I went nowhere, except out of the ministry.

John presently serves as a volunteer staff member with a seminary friend.

CHAPTER 6

So What Do They Want Anyway?
Multiple Expectations

"Handling people need not be so difficult…all you need is inexhaustible patience, unfailing insight, unshakable stability, an unbreakable will, decisive judgment, inflatable physique, irrepressible spirit, plus unfeigned affection for all people and an awful lot of experience," Eric Webster.

"It's just thousands of expectations … some of them you don't even know they expected of you until after they're disappointed." That's how one frustrated pastor put it. He spoke for thousands of pastors, objects of the multiple and often contradictory hopes, wants, beliefs, wishes and fancies of the people they serve. People who construct an image of a pastor using their differing definitions, their experiences, their assumptions, their needs, their desires, even their earlier disappointments, leaving pastors asking, "So what do they want anyway?"

It was between Sunday morning services. I went to my study with my pulpit robe still on. I opened the back door to get a little fresh air. A mother and her young son were playing on the grass as I walked out. The boy looked up to see this black robed figure whom he had never seen up close before. "Hello, G—" he said, catching himself. "I mean pastor," he continued. Momentarily, he was confused. We laugh and excuse the little boy's misspeak. But in view of the expectations laid on a pastor by those who know better, you would think they thought you were a part of the Godhead.

Not that having expectations of a pastor is wrong. The Bible's definition of the pastoral role is filled with God's expectations of you and me. It is the "thousands of expectations." It is expectations based in projections, putting on the present pastor the characteristics of a previous pastor. Or in these days of TV ministries, the charisma of a David Jeremiah or Joyce Meyer and others form the image projected onto the pastor of First Unspectacular Church of Horsehead, North Dakota. Given the mobility of Americans, people moving from a prosperous church in, say, Dallas to Horsehead, bring expectations with them that are unreasonable, if not impossible, for the small town church.

The sentient values of congregational members form part of their expectations. These are the quiet, unwritten and unspoken, often cultural ways a church works. Never codified in the constitution, by-laws or mission statement, they are nonetheless important to the membership. "We only use whipped cream, not Cool Whip in this church," was an unspoken rule of one rural church. "The pastor always checks with Uncle Harold (the unelected leader of the church, a term used by Lyle Schaller) before he brings up a matter to the Board." These are unwritten rules but the pastor better know them after a few months in any particular ministry.

There are people who measure success in terms of George Barna's *ABC's of Ministry, Attendance, Buildings and Cash*. Some measure success in institutional terms, a new constitution, a new marriage manual and new pews and expect the pastor to be as interested or uninterested as they are. For some, success is meeting these expectations.

Expectations stretch beyond church life, though. The pastor is idealized as the model Christian, the perfect spouse and parent, hail fellow well-met. He sometimes succeeds in reaching (or appears to reach) some idealized expectations of him or her and too often he begins to believe it. I believed it once and it was disastrous.

Whatever expectations a pastor adopts, they will shape his identity in that congregation. Before you accept a call, find out about their expectations of you and ask yourself whether or not they fit with your life mission, interests, competencies and style. As a pastor you will be defined by those multiple expectations, hidden assumptions, unfounded suppositions and "generous" advice.

1. Know yourself

The picture we carry around of ourselves can get us into trouble, especially if it includes meeting every expectation placed on us. We need to know our strengths and our weaknesses, where we can be effective and where we cannot be. We need to know our limitations and we must know and celebrate our gifts. Henri Nouwen wrote about "feeling at home in our own skin." In part that means knowing ourselves for who we really are. Nothing makes expectations harder to live with than when we think we can fulfill all of them but have neither the interest, ability, training or other personal traits needed to do so. Take the PRO-D survey (www.taiinc.com) and discover who you are.

2. Accept yourself

When diverse expectations meet with low self-esteem, it can be very stressful. When you attempt to be "all things to all people" because you are insecure, equating your worth with performance, you're in trouble. We are told to "love your neighbor *as yourself.*" We must value ourselves if we are to value and serve others aright… and not be intimidated by every expectation laid on us.

3. Be honest and forthright

Many expectations are laid on a pastor to fill a vacuum his/her forthrightness should have spoken to earlier. It is not helpful to a congregation to have a pastor who knows and accepts himself but seldom, if ever, shares who he is with them. As a pastor I found that people identify most readily with a pastor who will be straightforward and transparent about his weaknesses and strengths. Tell the congregation what you can and cannot do, what you have little desire to do, your successes and your failures. Before you are asked to be superman, let them know you are not.

Express your call to ministry periodically. You told the search group at your first interview. Tell the story of it every year or so to the congregation. People need to know you are a pastor by divine appointment. You are serious about God's expectations. The great preacher Peter Marshall did so in his sermon "Touch on the Shoulder." The anniversary of your call to ministry or the day you first came to the church you serve could be a good time to talk about your call to ministry and what you have learned in your last year serving with them.

4. Consider a customized covenant

While a covenant will not cover every expectation, many of them through inclusion or exclusion can be clarified by spelling out what the congregation expects from the pastor and the pastor from the congregation. In an old joke Mason says to Dixon, "You've got to draw the line somewhere." Covenants draw lines.

5. Ask

A pastor may not meet all the requirements of a congregation, but how can he if he does not ask once in a while what is expected of him. Early on, when he/she is a learner more than a leader, it is wise to inquire of the leadership what are their anticipations. You may not be able or even willing to meet every expectation, but at least ask! You'll avoid the sorrow of the pastor who said he didn't know what was expected of him until after the congregants were disappointed.

6. Empower others

Where pastors cannot effectively serve, God has people in the church who can. The church, after all, is an amalgam of spiritually gifted people serving as different parts of the Body "so that the body of Christ may be built up…" (Eph. 4:12). Lacking in any strength does not mean that the church overall lacks that strength. In the words of the Lord to Moses, "Let my people go" (Exod. 7:16). It is how God expects his church to appear… a proper functioning of all its parts. Empower others to do what you cannot.

7. Set intentional goals

Goals make clear a year's expectations, leaving certain wishes of the body to be completed at other times. "Yes, we can do that but you'll have to bring it up next year when we set new goals." How many times have I put off expectations by appealing to the need to meet already determined expectations! Bad ideas are often forgotten by the next year.

Furthermore, "when there is no vision, the people are scattered" (Prov. 29:18). When you don't know where you are going, people are scattered, can I say scatter-brained? Such a congregation restlessly multiplies expectations and the pastor gets caught in the maelstrom.

8. Listen

No one knows or fulfills his calling perfectly. Everyone has the need of others to know what his task is. To fulfill God's calling, all of us need the rest of us. Seneca wrote, "I suppose that many might have attained to wisdom, had they not thought they had already attained it." Dismissing the expectations of others presupposes we need not listen; we have it down perfectly already.

> *"A wise old owl sat in an oak; the more he saw the less he spoke;*
> *the less he spoke the more he heard; why aren't we like that old bird."*
> —Edward Hersey Richards

9. Let God speak through the expectations of others

Every pastor must affirm that the circumstances of life do not make or break us. It is how we respond to those circumstances. Could it be that God is speaking in the voice of a seasoned church member expressing an expectation of you? Do "all things work together for good" or only the good things? (Rom. 8:28). A piece of Haiku poetry goes, "My barn having burned down, I can now see the moon." A loss can be a gain. What you reject off-hand may be what you need to take in-hand. Is God speaking?

10. Honor your predecessors

Previous pastors had strengths you do not have and you have abilities and gifts they did not. As I wrote earlier, people tend to project the strength of a previous pastor as their expectations of you. Speak of him/ her positively; it will not reflect negatively on you. If you do, it may surprise you how accepting a congregation will be of shortcomings you have or expectations you don't meet.

CONCLUSION

There are expectations in every part of life. Expectations in every job. Your spouse, family, community, country, all have their expectations of you. So expect expectations. In the many, contradictory, impossible expectations, real and imagined, don't be perplexed; be prepared. Protect yourself against overcommitment and the loss of what God has called you to do. Unless, of course, the pastorate is no longer the future you desire or the purpose Christ has for your life.

Fifty-seven percent of pastors have considered quitting because of the overwhelming job demands, according to David Bryant.

MY STORY—CALVIN

What is my story? After serving the LORD as a missionary and pastor, I was in transition without a place to serve. I was invited to candidate at a church that was without a pastor for over two years. They were earnest about finding a leader. The search committee invited me to come and meet with them and to preach. It was a good weekend. A unanimous call to be their pastor was extended to me. I accepted the invitation, we moved and I became their new pastor.

Little did I know that the "power people" in the church were watching my wife and me. They wanted their new pastor to quickly turn things around and increase the number of attendees. I initiated training programs on how to share your faith and how to study the Bible and apply God's Word to their lives. New people began attending and were added to the church. After two and a half years the largest number of new members ever for this church were welcomed into its life on a Sunday morning, followed by a reception after the evening service. God had blessed the church and there was great cause for thanksgiving.

Unknown to me, on that same evening, a secret meeting was called by several of the church members. The meeting was to discuss the "concerns" of the church with the elders. A list of "concerns" (basically against my wife and me) were made and given to the elders. On Monday morning, an elder called and asked if he could meet me after lunch. He shared the results of the secret meeting with me. I was stunned and asked a few questions for clarification. Did those with a "concern" want to meet with me and discuss the matter? After a few days of thinking and praying, I met with our leaders and offered to confer with those who had the "concerns" but they were not willing to do so.

I sought counsel from friends and took it to the pastoral committee of the presbytery. The committee from presbytery came to the church and spoke with some of the members. What was surfacing in the church was a pattern of how the church had failed to work with members who expressed "concerns" with former pastors. They sought a quick solution. Remove the pastor and the problem will disappear.

The consensus of the pastoral committee was that the problem was present before I arrived. I was not part of the problem or part of the solution and I should peacefully resign. My wife and I decided that we would take the counsel of the pastoral committee and resign. With six months' severance pay we put our house up for sale and began our search for a future ministry. The day we settled on our house was the same time we received our last paycheck. We then put our things in storage and moved from Atlanta to Virginia Beach with our children.

In Virginia Beach, we visited various churches and finally settled in one that had been highly recommended by a pastor friend. The first day we visited I filled out the visitor's card and soon received a call from one of the members of the church. He was thanking us for our visit and then explained the various programs in the church that might be of interest to us. I told him I was a pastor in transition and his response was, "I think that we have something for you." I could not believe what he said and asked him to send me some information. Soon after, I received the pamphlet, "Pastor-in-Residence." After reading it over, I found that the church had a special program for exited pastors. I called the church and made an appointment to speak with the pastor who had developed this ministry that stood beside pastors in transition.

After my interview with this leader, I was invited to consider becoming a "Pastor-in-Residence" at that church. Once my wife and I accepted the invitation we met with the leadership of the church and shared "our journey." There was a covenant made with the church for a six-month period to oversee our restoration process. On Sunday my wife and I were introduced to the congregation and gave a brief testimony. We were then installed as a Pastor-in-Residence. During my time serving with the church, I shared my burden for fellow pastors who had been pushed from Christ's calling. The church became a "home church" for us. Week by week as we attended worship services, God used His Word to encourage and restore us. The relationship with the church and the leadership was very supportive. As a Pastor-in-Residence with the church, we assisted with visitation, teaching and preaching. At the end of our time in the Pastor- in-Residence program the senior pastor asked me to consider helping them take the Pastor-in-Residence ministry nationwide.

CHAPTER 7

What The Role
Is Called Up Yonder

"…discharge all the duties of your ministry."
Paul to Timothy

"My resignation is a protest," wrote the Reverend Max Morris in the *Miami Herald*. "…a protest against a concept of the ministry which forces the Pastor to be an executive, an administrator, an organizational genius, a public relations expert, a confessor to hundreds of people who have 'stumped their toes' and 'nicked their fingers' and need a sympathetic shoulder on which they can cry —more seriously, a one-man complaint department for disgruntled people who are at war within and are constantly causing wars without."

Another pastor wrote, "Too many people look to the clergy to be personal managers, financiers, ad hoc business managers, errand boys, counselors, general do-gooders, and angels—ad nauseum."

"I am appalled at what is required of me," wrote a clergyman and quoted by Barbara Gibson, "I am supposed to move from sickbed to administrative meeting, to planning, to supervising, to counseling, to praying, to troubleshooting, to budgeting, to audio systems, to meditation, to worship preparation, to newsletter, to staff problems, to mission projects, to conflict management, to community leadership, to study, to funerals, to weddings, to preaching. I am supposed to be 'in charge' but not *too* in charge, administrative executive, sensitive pastor, skillful counselor, public speaker, spiritual guide, politically savvy, intellectually sophisticated. And I am expected to be superior, or at least first rate, in all of them. I am not supposed to be depressed, discouraged, cynical, angry, or hurt. I am supposed to be upbeat, positive, strong, willing, available. Right now I am not filling any of those expectations very well. And I am tired."

The confusion and conflict surrounding a pastor's role is part of the stuff with which pastors live. They juggle an ever-present multitude of ambiguous and often incongruous roles and expectations. They suffer little identity crises periodically as they try to find the role blend most acceptable to their congregations. Dean Hoge said in *Pastors in Transition*, "Ministers are at risk for emotional burnout due to the multiple roles they must fulfill and the pressures they feel from all sides."

In a survey asking how exited pastors experienced stress in their ministry, role conflict was a top-ranked producer of stress second only to conflict over how ministry was to be done in the church. Role ambiguity, multiplicity and a general failure to define and restate it to the congregation are the blows that repeatedly have put pastors in torment while they serve. These also place them in danger of visits from leadership with the "news" they are no longer pastor... period!

The three worlds of role conflict

First, there is conflict among those outside the pastor himself as to how he is to function. Divergent role definitions and expectations exist among and between significant others who surround the pastor (superiors, peers in ministry, congregational lay leadership/membership). They do not agree among themselves about a pastor's role. The pastor gets caught between these differing authority sources and how they define the clergy role.

Second, there is conflict between the norms and values internalized by the pastor himself and those of his work situation. Studies show that young pastors in particular leave seminary valuing the scholar role while the churches to which they go want them to be church promoters. Pastors tend to see themselves as change agents while lay people tend to see their churches as havens from change. This internal-external tension leaves the pastor spending much of his time doing what he values least, pressured by divergent expectations.

Third, conflict among the internalized norms, models and motives of the pastor himself. He has certain incompatible though equal values and expectations of himself, setting up within him a struggle over the satisfactory performance of his job. For example, he may value the demurring, self-denying servant role, but also have internalized achievement as a value demanding assertive, bold and controlling approaches to ministry. Both imperatives call out to him and an internal struggle ensues. He wants resolution or thinks resignation.

What churches and pastors see as the most important roles of a pastor (a comparison)

In a survey of thirty-three exited pastors, the following roles were, in the opinion of these pastors, considered by the churches they served as very important compared with what they personally saw as essential:

	Church	Pastor
Worship Leader	72%	88%
Teacher	71%	100%
Church Promoter	63%	15%
Scholar	16%	39%
Preacher	88%	91%
Evangelist	59%	47%
Administrator	55%	30%
Gen. Practitioner	52%	53%

More important to the church than to their pastors, in the judgment of these exited pastors, was the role of church promoter, evangelist and administrator. More important to the pastors than to their church, again in the judgment of these exited pastors, was worship leader, teacher, scholar and preacher (that is what pastors enjoy the most, right?). Obviously, the pastoral roles envisioned by churches as most important are quite different from how pastors understand the most important roles they play. The number surveyed as well as some of the differing percentages is small but the results leave us asking whether or not the different assumptions between church and pastor regarding roles may have been one of the reasons why these pastors left ministry. Unclear and conflicting role definitions put a pastor at risk.

In a survey I did when first becoming interested in exited pastors I noticed such a difference between how young pastors, just having completed seminary, varied in their understanding of their role compared to what the congregation calling them considered to be their role. I went to a college professor who taught statistical analysis and asked her to examine the matter. She applied what she called Chi-Square analysis to the numbers; her conclusion was that the numbers indicated a vast gulf between pastors and churches in terms of a pastor's role. Young pastors approached their task, just having been professionalized by teachers who unpacked heavy and hard theological issues, and the pastor's instinct was to do the same with his congregation. In the meantime, the congregation was simply asking, "When are you going to put this church high on the community map?" The young pastor was most comfortable with digging up theological roots for his people while the people were far more interested in public relations, attractive and entertaining worship services and the pastor getting his name wherever he could in the community to, as they said, "put the church on the map." In both instances, the role of pastors had little reference to "what the role is called up yonder." Some have speculated that it is this difference in understanding a pastor's role that accounts for generally shorter first pastorates.

A minister who serves within this web of ambiguous and incongruous role definitions and priorities will attempt to discover what the role is called up yonder. He will ask how God defines the role he is to live out.

How God defines the role

A pastor asks what characterized the ministry of the Chief Shepherd and thus serves as a model to him. He will attempt to work through the meaning of his call, his gifts, and his ordination. Oswald Chambers said, "Continually relate to yourself what the purpose of your life is." What did God call you to be? A pastor must define and redefine what it means to be a pastor and choose which of these are his model and priority roles.

- Servant (Mark 10:15; 1 Cor. 3:5) In subjection to Christ; attendant to God's people
- Pastor/Teacher (Eph. 4:11) Skilled instruction and training with care and vigilance
- Preacher/Encourager (2 Tim. 4:2; Acts 20:20, 27) Persuasive, stimulating to duty, counsel
- Shepherd (Isa. 40:11; Acts 20:28) Tender care and vigilance

- Witness/Evangelist (Acts 1:8, 20, 24, 31; 2 Tim. 4:5) To bring good news; proclamation as a herald
- Steward (1 Cor. 4:1, 2) Manager of a household, guardian
- Ambassador (2 Cor. 5:22) Representative of another government
- Disciple(r) (Matt. 28:19) Learner, teacher, follower
- Overseer (1 Tim. 3:1-7) Look over, exercising oversight
- Elder (1 Tim. 5:17) Mature spiritual experience and understanding
- Equipper (Eph. 4:11-13) Prepare people for the work of ministry

A pastor must never settle for a definition of his role less than what God has called him to be. The same is true of the church he serves. He will gently force the question of his identity on the congregation, insisting that such a definition falls within the margins of biblical boundaries. He will develop a capacity for balancing role demands within himself, and between himself and the congregation. He will accept his limitations and recognize that in him "God has chosen the foolish things of the world to shame the wise, and God has chosen the weak things of the world to shame the strong" (1 Cor. 1:26-29). By accepting his personal limitations, he accepts both the limitations and expansiveness of his role and will choose priorities. He will consider the character dimensions of biblical designations. He will work out what the role is within the changing context of his present life and ministry. He will recognize the multiplicity, ambiguity and conflict in role definitions and will, therefore, always have on his personal agenda the pursuit of what it means to be a minister in his present place and time. He will nurture his calling by speaking of it often and telling what it means in the context of the church he serves.

When he translates titles into concrete actions, he will be careful to justify his actions by the definition of his role. Whatever he is asked to do or become, he will test that suggested action against how the Scriptures define the pastoral role; while he may go beyond it, the priorities for his life and work will be the roles God's Word has called him to play.

CONCLUSION

People assign roles to their pastors that are often ambiguous, conflicting and sometimes beyond what is justifiable biblically. Pastors take on roles and responsibilities that are based in conflicting ideals held by them. A wise pastor will remember his call and rehearse it periodically before his leadership. A wise pastor chooses his role priorities in every situation to which he is called but always within the boundaries of God's Word. A wise pastor will learn and keep on learning what the role is called up yonder. Otherwise, he may put himself at risk, exposed to the possibility of no future in the church. He may feel safe doing what the church has asked him to be and do but if it is not the role called up yonder, he is not safe at all.

Many at-risk pastors have diminished the role to which they are called. I suggest strongly that you take several days to ask:

Am I sure I am called to ministry? Consider your call.

What is the biblical role of a pastor?

How does that role compare with the role I now play in the church? If I find discrepancies in this comparison, what can I do about it?

Does God bless the pastor who knows who he is and is to be and is courageous enough to be just that?

Where with sensitivity can I get started redefining the pastoral role as taught in Scripture?

MY STORY

A Pastor's Prayer

"I could have sold most anything
But you called me to be a pastor.
And here I sit among the people;
Pushing prayers, Swapping jokes,
Trading self-esteem for longevity
Begging for building funds,
Rustling a Catholic now and then
Hawking the urban problems
Picking pockets with committees and boards
Pirating among the open pulpits
Auctioning God to the lowest bidder;
Lord, just exactly what was it you had in mind
when we talked so long ago?
Would you please go over it just one more time?

Dr. Norman Shawchuck
Leading the Congregation 1993
Abingdon Press
Used by Permission

CHAPTER 8

Listed In "Who's Through"

Many of us know people listed in *Who's Who in America*. Leafing through "Who's Who" recently, I began to think of another book not yet written. We could call it *Who's Through in America*?

Few pastors are listed in "Who's Who." However, if there was a *Who's Through* book I could list a dozen pastors within minutes, pastors first at risk then forced to resign their church posts, never to return to vocational ministry again. Nearly 40 percent of exited pastors leave and never return, says John LaRue of *Christianity Today*. List them in *Who's Through*.

Pastors sometimes leave on their own. Some simply abandon their call. Some get tired of endless meetings. Some weary of the struggle not to be themselves. Some burn out. Some are confused about their role in the church. Some whose dreams of success never develop. Some lose faith. Some face false moral charges. Some feel neck-deep in guilt. Some are caught in the middle of church conflict. Not often found, I have worked with exited pastors who got addicted to gambling, to alcohol, to the "art" of photographing nudes, to plagiarizing sermons, to stealing the church's petty cash.

Many pastors do not decide on their own to leave. Others decide it for them. They are forced to resign.

Most never saw it coming. I've asked countless exited pastors why the church they served released them so suddenly, so unexpectedly. Nine out of ten answered, "I don't know why."

This book addresses the major at-risk factors that may answer the "Why?" question. Others are forced to resign for less dramatic reasons. Here are three such reasons:

I. It Has Been Very Difficult For Me To Say "No."

Dorothy Parker said of one of her acquaintances, "She speaks eighteen languages, but can't say 'no' in any of them." Most of us can only speak one or two languages but find it difficult nonetheless to say "no" anyway. This is particularly true of pastors. We feel guilty to refuse someone their request for our time, attention or help. We feel neglectful of our calling, derelict of duty; as if we are playing favorites should we not say "yes." Perhaps we are too insecure to refuse one of our "bosses" when he or she asks. What about not being able to do what is asked and not being willing to admit that we are less than superman? Perhaps we've built a "bionic minister" image and saying "no" weakens that image. Maybe we don't know what alternatives to suggest so we take on the request ourselves. Have we had a bad experience saying "no" once and are frightened of ever repeating that experience again? Perhaps we value a servanthood that defines itself as doing everything we are asked. It's possible that we do not want to share power, or do not have a biblical idea of spiritual gifts present in others and not all gifts in us. Do we know what God has called us to be and do? Have we a clear idea of "what the role is called up yonder," our identity as God defines it?

In one survey of pastors, all of the top nine at-risk pastors said it was difficult for them to say "no." In another survey of 101 pastors, 60 said "Sometimes," "Quite Often" or "Most of the Time" as their response to the same difficulty. Can this be a major reason for the epidemic of exited pastors we experience in America? How right Josh Billings was over a century ago, "One-half of the troubles of this life can be traced to saying yes too quickly and not saying no soon enough."

Not being able to say "No," we soon get overworked, a first step to burnout. What can we do?

A. Set a clear vision and annual goals

"Without a vision the people are scattered," that is, they are going off in all different directions, suggesting a myriad of ideas without reference to what should have captured the heart and soul of the congregation, in other words, a guiding vision. Vision is expansive but also narrowing. Remember, "If it doesn't fit, you've got to acquit." In such a case, if it doesn't fit the vision, you must say "no."

George Ordiorne of Management By Objective said, "People get so enmeshed in activity that they lose sight of the purpose of their work." It's called the Activity Trap. The key to church accomplishment is vision and goals with activities geared to that vision. Saying "no" depends on having vision and goals and not being so enmeshed in activity that people feel free to suggest more and more activities.

Annual goals define what the church will be and do in the year ahead. Many times I have said, "Maybe we can make that part of next year's goals." If it is just a whim and not of the Spirit's leading, it is often forgotten in next year's planning. You need not say "no," if you are able to say "yes, but…"

B. Develop a "relaxed concern" strategy

Frank Tillapaugh used this term to connote the pastor's role when new ideas are suggested and developed. You need not say "no" but that the ministry suggested be developed by the one who suggests it, by finding others in the congregation with a similar burden and that together the ministry develop. If the suggestion is not the burden of others and does not develop, God has said "no." If it does develop, the pastor has empowered the people to act out their gifts and calling and he becomes not the initiator or maintainer of what his congregation does but its overseer, a proper role for pastors.

C. Earn the authority you are given

Elders rule. An elder is to rule well. His character and demeanor are clearly spelled out (1 Tim. 5:17; Tit. 1:5-9). A pastor (elder) can be disqualified (1 Cor. 9:27). Certainly not unilaterally does he rule, but among all that he agrees to in the denomination he serves, he is asked, "Are you now willing to take the charge of this church, agreeable to your declarations when accepting their call?" Pastors are commanded, "not lording it over those entrusted to you." They rule by being "examples to the flock" (1 Pet. 5:3). In this a pastor earns what by gift and calling he is given. Leadership demands a life worthy of managing the household of God. It may not be easy to say "no" but if you have earned the right to do so by earning the authority you have been given, "no" is received without animus.

D. Practice saying "no"

Hear yourself say the word in private and it won't shock you when you hear yourself saying it to a church member. I like the English proverb that goes, "Make yourself all honey, and the flies will devour you." If "no" is not in your vocabulary, you lose credibility, command and capital with the congregation. Charles Haddon Spurgeon said, "Learn to say 'no,' it will be of more use to you than to be able to read Latin." So practice saying the word out loud. Stop now and say "no" a hundred times. Look into a mirror and watch yourself mouth it. If you know you will have to say "no" some particular day, say it a hundred times before you leave your house in the morning.

My wife visited her doctor with what felt like a stomach tied in knots. Being a pastor's wife was stressful, as every spouse of a pastor knows.

She was sure he would give her a prescription for the latest anti-stress medication. He handed her the script and she looked at it. This was his prescription: "Just say No." She did as he said and within a short time she was herself again. "No" is more than good for your soul; it is good for your body as well.

II. I Keep Trying To Please Everybody.

The congregation was ecstatic when Skaar accepted their invitation to be their pastor. The community and congregation were almost entirely Swedish in heritage... and their new pastor was right from the old country. His stories charmed them. His accent reminded them of their grandparents who had come themselves from "gamla landet." To every event for 100 miles around where Swedes gathered he was asked to come, to pray, and to sing in the heavenly language they were sure God understood best.

All that goodwill lasted almost four wonderful years. You would have thought the congregation would want Skaar as pastor forever. But that was not to be. Quite suddenly and painfully for Skaar, the congregational leadership asked him to resign. He hung his head and quietly moved out of town without another place to serve.

I asked him why he was forced out of the church that had loved him for so long. I shall never forget his answer. "I tried to please everybody." So pleased with him at the start, he thought pleasing the congregation was key to his success in America. Having been taught that pleasing them was what they should expect from Skaar, their pleasure now was to demand his "good-bye."

"Most pastors are people-pleasers," said H.B. London. Call it wanting to be liked. Call it charm. Call it being agreeable. But trying to always please is more than being pleasant. It is a vain hope, a no-win effort, often little more than an ego trip, sweet at first but bitter in the end. It is often flattery and even pastors "flatter others for their own advantage," (Jude 16), "and a flattering mouth works ruin" (Prov. 26:28). It is deception (Ps. 12:2). It is not benign, but a cancer at its root.

A few thoughts on the penchant to please everybody:

A. *Please God as your first priority*

God cannot be charmed, deceived or flattered. Pleasing Him is bodies made living sacrifices "pleasing to God" (Rom.12:1). It is making fragrant offerings, "pleasing to God" (Phil. 4:18). It is upright prayer (Prov. 15:8). It is children obedient to their parents "for this pleases the Lord" (Col. 3:20). It is "living peaceful and quiet lives in godliness and holiness" for "this pleases God our Savior" (1 Tim. 2:2, 3). It is living by faith "without which it is impossible to please God" (Heb. 11:6). It is honesty "dishonest scales do not please him" (Prov. 20:23). "Make it a goal to please Him" (2 Cor. 5:9). It's remarkable how the penchant to always please others loses strength when we make it our goal to please Him first. A good exercise is to ask, "Am I now trying to win the approval of others, or God?" (Gal. 1:10). Yes, we should please our neighbor but "for his good, to build him up" (Rom. 15:1). We attempt to please everybody but "so that they may be saved" (1 Cor. 10:33). Please others but for the right reasons. Pleasing others for the right reasons pleases God.

Eric Lindell, the Olympic gold medalist, said in an interview, "When I am running, I always feel the pleasure of God." How wonderful it would be if in the preaching/teaching, worship leading, and corporate prayer ministries in which we participate we could feel the pleasure of God.

B. *Be absolutely certain that God loves and accepts you*

On good days and bad. On Mondays as well as Sundays. Even when you are bent on pleasing everybody. Whether the congregation loves you or not.

Being unsure that we are loved and accepted as we are, others become the mirrors into which we look to see our value. It's important to us that they return a good reflection. That they tell we are worthwhile. Maybe the best pastor they have ever had? What fairly well guarantees that? Please them. Needing people to tell him he is OK, he indulges them, amuses them and charms them. To do so is thought to promise the love for which he hungers. When I see a pastor making sure everybody is pleased, doing nothing unless at least the major players in the church are happy, a big red flag goes up reading "INSECURE." That pastor has little experiential and emotional understanding of God's unconditional, unearned, undeserved, unchangeable love and acceptance. Fixed and firm. Unshakable and unwavering. An open and shut case.

Martin Luther said that the number one sin is unbelief. Applied to the unconditional love of God for you, not to believe it is unbelief.

I know Skaar. He often impresses me as looking for love in all the wrong places. Skaar, God loves you the way you are.

C. Be a leader, pleasing or not

Pastors who attempt to please everyone lead with a finger to the wind. Mistakenly, they think this is caring or trying to be relevant or being humble. He is attempting to lead from the middle of the pack, when a leader is out in front with vision and energy taking his followers to the mountaintop of spiritual maturity. Congregations want and expect that quality in the one they entrust with the privilege of being their leader.

There is good and bad leadership. A leader with little more than the title does not gain followers, at least for long. There is to be a quality to his leadership that, whether he pleases people or not, is the leadership that keeps him out of the at-risk zone.

III. I Need To Prove Myself A Hard Worker.

Walking down the main street of Junction City, Kansas, with the pastor of one of its good churches, we walked double time, to say the least. "Why are we walking so fast?" I asked him. I shall always remember his reply, "Whenever I'm out like this, I want to look like I'm going somewhere to do something for God. So I walk fast."

We stayed overnight in Kansas City with a pastor and his family. We awoke about six in the morning hearing him running down the hallway and clearing his throat. When he got to the front living room, we could hear him open the shade letting in the early sunshine. When we got up a couple hours later, I asked why he got out of bed so early and put up the front shade and then returned to bed. "Because at about six one of my deacons goes by the house on his way to work, and I want him to think I'm up and working already." And of all things, he had a contract with his church calling for him to only work forty hours a week.

In a survey I did "proving myself a hard worker" was tenth in a list of forty-two factors the pastors taking the survey could have marked describing their present church experience. In the top nine with scores indicating they were at-risk pastors, eight said they had to prove themselves hard workers. Does the pastor profession have a reputation all of us try to live up to? We are hard workers! Do we rely on character or charades, the Spirit or spin, anointing or acting?

A. Be honest with the congregation

If your style of ministry includes trying to prove you work hard, at least tell your leadership that you are prone to do that. They may well be struck with the maturity of your self- understanding. You will find, too, that your source of power is that in which you cannot glory. Paul wrote, "…for when I am weak, then I am strong" (2 Cor. 12:10). Rather than the acknowledgement of your humanness weakening your power as a minister, it adds to it. It touches something deep in people and they say, "Ah, this pastor says what we know ourselves to be both strengths and weaknesses, overcoming and despairing, light and darkness. I can follow him."

B. Acknowledge rest as part of the Gospel

Jesus said, "Come to me... and I will give you rest . . . you will find rest for your souls" (Matt. 11:28, 29). Spiritual rest, you say. Yes, but can the soul be at ease if the body is perpetually up tight? Jesus also said to his disciples, "Come with me... and get some rest"(Mark 6:31). There is no excuse for laziness, but there is a mandate for rest.

C. Practice proving what God asks us to prove

First, we must prove our repentance by our deeds (Acts 25:20). Acts of obedience declare our repentance to be genuine. Second, we are to prove ourselves faithful to the trust we have been given (1 Cor. 4:2). Practice proving your repentance and your faithfulness and you will prove all that God expects you to prove.

For years I wore a gold ring given to me by a friend in India. Engraved on it were the initials N.W.G.P. They were the initials of my friend's full name (his last name was Prasad). Wearing the ring reminded me of my friend and the need in India, but I had to change the meaning of those initials to what would mean something to me. So I did... and scores of times I looked at it to remind me that "Nothing Wickman Gotta Prove."

CONCLUSION

A black Cadillac was parked at a 5-star hotel near the Los Angeles airport. The owner had apparently changed jobs and could now afford a luxury car. I was interested particularly in his vanity license plate. It read: WAS REV. He apparently had left behind his "reverend" profession... and I wondered how it happened. Perhaps he had never learned to say "No," or wanted to please everybody or thought he had to prove himself a hard worker. At any rate, he "was rev," just like many others at risk, who take no steps to protect their future or guard their present.

MY STORY—ANONYMOUS

Having grown up in the ministry as a pastor's son, I was already prepared for forced exits. We had experienced two of them from churches. I expected it to happen in my first church and it almost did. I did not expect it to happen in my second church. I had confidence, experience and was being the church leader I needed to be. I could be the youth leader, music director as well as Senior Pastor. I couldn't say "No" to anything that needed to be done. Looking back, there are some things I would have done differently. I would have been kinder, gentler and have treated people better than I did once or twice. But overall, there were no charges of any wrongdoing. It was a chemistry mismatch in a church where the pastors were usually grown from within the congregation and the community. I was an outsider and got the boot.

When it came, it was a shock. I tried to stop it. I delayed it. But on a cold January night, the church was to take a vote to either accept or reject me as their leader. A two-thirds majority was needed: fifty-seven votes. The vote was counted three times. It came to exactly fifty-seven. I heard a door click shut. It was God calling me out of that church.

We left with hearts broken and there were tears. But ironically, they allowed me to stay on and minister for another six months, which I did with grace and peace. That proved to be the most productive time of all. We forgave them for this injustice of a forced exit. There was no severance pay —just a party and a gift. Then I walked out the door.

The recovery time was spent in a "safe-haven" at a church nearby. They nurtured us through the trial of the next year, which was spent worshipping there, and being overseen by a group of caregivers in the church who were committed to our recovery.

My wife maintained her job as an accountant. We lived in the same house. I began a house painting business and worked it for four years. In the meantime, I started planting a church—a great and fruitful experience in spite of the fact that it closed ten years later. I taught Christian high school for four years to support church planting. I am now in an interim position at my first church helping them through a turbulent time where their pastor was forced to resign. I am blessed that Pastor-in-Residence was there when I needed it. God used it and the graceful people of the church mightily to help us through.

I know the pain and shock of being asked to leave a congregation. Sometimes it is simply because of a mismatch between the church and its pastor. Sometimes it is painful beyond belief. His strength is enough for the hard times… but my prayer for you, dear reader, is that you will never have to experience a forced exit from the greatest work in all the world, pastor to the people of God.

Note: The writer of the above had all the training of a Doctor of Ministry degree from a good seminary; nonetheless, forced exit happened to him. Even though it happened twice to his father, he was still surprised by it happening to him.

CHAPTER 9

Not The Preacher We Wanted

"Preach the Word, be prepared…"
2 Timothy 4:2

Robert came to me having just been asked to leave the church as its pastor. He confessed not to know why he was asked to resign except that one of the elders who announced the "you're outta here" decision rather casually said, "You're not the preacher that you were when you first came." I asked him about his study habits, the titles of recent sermons, the time he took for preparation, including prayer, the books he was presently reading, if preaching was for him his foremost duty as a pastor. With weak study habits, Saturday night preparation, even some plagiarism, and more, Robert knew that the elder was right.

Martin confessed to me that his preaching was mostly the taped messages of Rick Warren, author of *The Purpose Driven Life*. When some of his congregants went to a Warren conference in California and heard Warren speak several times, they were surprised to hear what their pastor had been preaching all along, sometimes word for word. They returned home to confront their pastor with what he was doing and asked him to resign. I met him four years later as he finally became a pastor again.

A pastor in Kansas told me, "I can preach Billy Graham's sermons better than he can." It was not surprising that in a few years his church dwindled and he was asked to resign.

If you were to ask most church leadership why their last pastor was asked to resign, one of the answers you will hear is, "he was not the preacher we wanted (or needed, or we thought he was, or he thought he was, etc.)." In other words, most churches place a high value on preaching and many are often disappointed with the preaching/teaching they receive. In one survey I took, 88 percent of churches said preaching is the number one difference between an attractive church and just a church church.

Of course to some, good preaching is good oratory. To others, good preaching is many stories, a few funny lines and less than twenty-five minutes. To still others, preaching should be extemporaneous, loud and dramatic. To one congregation, it must be exposition, to another heavy on application, to a different group, it is poetic flourishes and no grammatical mistakes; it is newspaper as well as Scripture. All argue for sincerity. Perhaps good preaching is like art; you know it is good when you hear it.

When the eighteenth century Archbishop of Canterbury asked why actors seem to have no difficulty in making an impression on the audience while preachers frequently leave them cold, Thomas Belleston, the actor, answered, "Actors speak of things imaginary as if they were real while you preachers too often speak of things real as if they were imaginary."

Preaching at its best is a blend of thought, word, emotion, conviction, presence, gesture, place, congregation, timing, message and more, empowered and anointed by the Holy Spirit and appropriate to its hearers. It is "theology on fire," Scripture rightly divided, truth saturating the life of the preacher and proclaimed with authority. It makes the mind consider and the heart jump. This is the preaching that congregations desire and, if their pastor is much less, pastors of most evangelical churches are at risk.

It was said of one preacher, "He had the art of almost saying something." If that is the way a pastor's major task is judged by his congregation, he may well be at risk. Does your preaching command the love of your congregation or…?

It is not my intention here to provide a mini-course in homiletics. This is a plea for palatable preaching. In my experience, I have come to believe these seven things about the preaching people want and need:

- **People want biblical preaching.** They need to know what God says. "Preach the Word." Sometimes expository, sometimes topical but all the time biblical. Not simply informational, but transformational.
- **People want prepared preaching.** Not junk food, put together as quickly as a hamburger at McDonalds.
- **People want life-centered preaching.** Example, not empty words. It captures in its tone and tenor the pastor's personal experience with God. Listeners ask, "Does this speaker know God intimately and does this message come from deep within that relationship?"
- **People want relevant preaching.** Someone said you cannot put the same shoe on every foot. People want preaching that fits their present need. The speaker knows that "in every pew sits a broken heart" or that someone listening has a child strung out on drugs, or someone who has lost his job, or someone about to lose his house in foreclosure.

- **People want intense preaching.** The carrier of the message must be about to explode with his message. "Proclaim the message with intensity," reads 2 Timothy 4:2 (The Message Bible), not with hysterics and hype but with spiritual muscle and passion.
- **People want contemporary preaching.** Today's headlines. Today's words. Today's illustrations.
- **People want life-changing preaching.** "Challenge, warn, and urge…" (2 Tim. 4:2). Application, not just information. Not just "What" but also "So What?" "As pastor he re-speaks, re-visions the Gospel so that his congregation experiences the *word*, not mere words" (Eugene Peterson).

Underlying all this is that people want a preacher who is called of God to proclaim Christ and knows it in his soul. Periodically, the preacher reminds his congregation that he is a preacher by divine appointment. I heard a seminary chaplain say to his listeners before he preached, "I speak to you today as one called of God to 'preach Christ and Him crucified.'" I understand this is the way he intentionally began every message, reaffirming before his hearers as well as remembering himself that he spoke as one called of God to do so.

Beyond the call essential to being a carrier of the gospel to a congregation there is this essential, expressed by Robert Murray McCheyne, "My people's greatest need is my personal holiness." A pastor may be an ordinary preacher or even an extraordinary preacher, but his word in the long run is hollow unless and until it can be said, he takes time to be holy.

Nothing that I know secures a pastor more in his position and out of the at-risk zone than that he knows he is called of God, his life exudes a conspicuous holiness and his preaching is biblical, prepared, life-centered, relevant, intense, contemporary and life-changing. Such protects your future and guards your present.

CONCLUSION

A large church in the Midwest had a pastor who, unbeknown to most of his congregation, preached his Sunday sermon to an empty sanctuary every Saturday night. He did so not simply for practice but because he believed that the most important thing he did in ministry was to preach God's Word and by preaching first to himself he saturated his soul with his message and could go to the pulpit on Sunday with a fire burning to speak the Word for that day.

If preaching is just a sidebar in your work with the congregation, you are at risk.

MY STORY—ADDISON

As I understand it, you know what is happening to me and have asked that I tell my story in a page and a half at most. I'll try.

First, I am pastor to my third church since seminary. When I left the first church for the second, I thought I was as well prepared as any pastor could be. I had one, four-year stint behind me. I had enough experience to know what my weaknesses were. I had enough experience to be realistic about the church and enough experience to know some of the pitfalls I might meet. But I was mistaken. I worked hard, preached as best I could, and enjoyed four years of ministry. Then there was the fifth year. I began to lose the edge, began to not care as much as I had, could not resolve the conflict that arose between those who wanted us to grow where we were and those who thought we ought to start a new church. I wasn't the well-honed pastor I thought I was. When another church 100 or so miles away asked if I would be a candidate for the pulpit there, my wife and I thought this might be a move we should really consider.

We were called there and we took the call. We are there now and it's the fifth year of pastoring this congregation. It was the fifth year when I left my last church and it now being the fifth year here, I'm a little nervous.

What I think you know, Chuck, is that the charismatic church a couple of miles away got a new preacher recently and they say he is a captivating, energetic speaker. I know many in my congregation have visited there and one guy told me after one of my worst messages that he thought the new preacher had preached the best message he had ever heard, when he visited there. Frankly, I wanted to tell him to go to… well, go to hear him every week.

At the Board meeting last month, I was asked to preach more verse-by-verse sermons. And that led to a discussion of all my preaching. I think there is nothing more devastating than for people to question your preaching… and maybe when they do, it's time to move on. Am I just paranoid? How can I keep up with those fluent TV preachers or, for that matter, the tall steeple church pastors who always get the speaking assignment at our denominational meetings. I wish I could just press a button and be out of here.

I didn't mean to let my discouragement show. Guess I'm not the kind of preacher most people seem to want. So, Chuck, when you get your book published, maybe some churches wanting a good-hearted but mediocre preacher will read it and contact you for a recommendation. Remember me, O.K.?

CHAPTER 10

A Spouse Ready To Quit

"He must manage his own family well."
1 Timothy 3:4

He was pastor of one of the larger churches in town. I called him one Saturday afternoon from my motel room and promptly stuck my foot in my mouth. "Let's have lunch on Monday," I said, continuing, "And bring your wife along, if she's still with you."

Monday came and we met at one of the better restaurants in the city. The pastor came by himself. He had been at a denominational meeting 100 miles away the last half of the week before. He came home on Saturday and to his horror, came home to an empty house. All the furniture was gone, but more tragically his wife and baby were gone too. She was tired of being a pastor's wife so, while he was gone, she moved far away; rarely did he see her again.

The wedding was beautiful. I know, I was the best man. But the life that followed for her was not good. A dozen years in the fishbowl were about ten years too much for her. They became part of the statistic: 30-50 percent of clergy marriages end in divorce.

A majority of pastors' spouses surveyed said that the most destructive event that occurred in their marriage was the day they entered ministry, according to the compilation of statistics published by Shiloh Place Ministries. The same composition reports that 80 percent of spouses feel left out and unappreciated by church members. Eighty percent wish their spouses had chosen another profession. Eighty percent feel pressure to do things and be something that they really are not. If a spouse and family are unhappy, any pastor is at risk. If at risk becomes exit, all of my experience says it will be more difficult to persuade the spouse to seek a return than to convince the pastor to do so.

A pastor may not be burned out. The pastor's spouse may be. A pastor may not seem to be at risk. The pastor's spouse may be ready to bail. If the spouse splits, the pastor often quits. A wise pastor will understand the stressors felt by his/her spouse, if for no other reason than her stresses are his stresses and for her to be ready to quit is for him to be at risk.

In my files I found this, written by a pastor's wife:

"A minister's wife should be attractive, but not too much; have nice clothes, but not too nice; have a nice basic hairdo, but not too nice; be friendly, but not too friendly; be aggressive and greet everyone, especially visitors, but not too aggressive; intelligent, but not too intelligent, educated, but not too educated; down-to-earth, but not too much so; capable but not too capable; charming but not too charming; and be herself, but not openly! ...The biggest "not too"—she must be quiet when her husband, children or she, herself, is criticized."

This does not describe every pastor's spouse, I'm certain. However, while in many ways rewarding, being a pastor's wife is often a rose with thorns, beauty with ashes, and sweet but with an undertone of sourness. Let's discuss the stresses of being a pastor's spouse.

1. **Unwritten Expectations**. Some churches expect the pastor's spouse to sing in the choir or play the organ, lead the women's ministry, do Vacation Bible School, have members over for dinner, keep her husband neatly dressed, make sure the kids are angels, never hold an outside job, live happily in a parsonage with worn carpets and more. Eighty percent of pastors' wives feel pressured to do things and be something in the church that they really are not and have no desire to do. The expectations will be many. The pastor's spouse should simply be herself.

2. **Finances.** "You keep him humble; we'll keep him poor." An overstatement, no doubt, but churches have the reputation of giving its pastors almost poverty wages. The spouse, whose job it is to manage a household on such a salary, feels the stress of it. Someone said that to a pastor's wife a twenty dollar bill is foreign currency. Most say, as Kate Mostel once said, "I didn't want to be rich. I just wanted enough to get the couch reupholstered." Proverbs 30:8 puts it, "...give me neither poverty nor riches, but give me only my daily bread."

3. **Being in the Middle.** Church members, rather than talking directly with the pastor, will talk to the pastor's spouse about issues of concern and complaint. She is expected to pass it on to her husband. Thus she serves in the awkward position of go-between.

4. **Little Family Time.** After working long hours, her pastor/husband neglects his family. The spouse becomes mother and part-time father. While the pastor/husband talks about quality time, the fact is his family needs quantity time. How ironic that a

pastor will preach on supportive husbands and loving wives and spend most of the week's hours away from her and the children.

5. **Insecurity.** Statistics about pastoral exodus are known to her. The possibility of what someone called receiving "the left foot of fellowship" keeps her insecure. A move may be imminent, initiated by board or bishop or by her restless husband.

6. **No Pastor.** Where does she go, when she needs pastoral counsel? Who will pray with her when she goes to the hospital? How delighted my wife was when an associate pastor visited her after surgery, saying to me, "I never had a pastor before."

7. **The Goldfish Bowl life.** Their life is open to everyone. The children are watched for any deviant behavior. She must pretend that her husband is near perfect when he is far from it. It's <u>1984</u> every day of every year.

8. **Loneliness.** In a survey of more than 200+ pastors' wives, taken by Fuller Seminary, 45 percent of them said they had no close friends in the church they serve. When their husbands are criticized, they have no understanding confidant to listen to them. Loneliness is especially critical when the pastor's wife hears her children criticized and needs to explode somewhere safe. Her husband's busy life and too little quality time with her and the children add to her deepening loneliness.

Given these stresses, a pastor has a responsibility to his spouse beyond what is ordinarily expected of him. Assuming that we are talking about a wife, avoiding the risk of losing it all means…

1. **Give her a good marriage.** A pastor will be at risk if his wife is unhappy in her marriage and his ministry. If a pastor is not to be at risk, he must give her a good marriage.

You must love her in words and in those actions that define love (1 Cor. 13). My wife sometimes says to me, "Do you love me or do you not; you told me once, but I forgot." She must be secure in your love, so tell her you love her. You must accept her as she is. You must listen to her fears, her aspirations, her joys, her struggles, her opinions, her changes, her silence. You must talk to her, not arguing or defending yourself when she talks about you. You must seek her greatest good and put her needs and interests above your own.

It is often said that if the wife is unhappy the whole family is unhappy. Therefore, a pastor may be at risk because his wife is unhappy in marriage and in ministry. The question then becomes, if a pastor wishes not to be at risk, what must he be as the pastor/husband to his spouse?

2. **Encourage her to be honest about her place in the church.** A member said to my wife shortly after our arrival at a new assignment, "I think you must be good with children." In her opinion Faith ought to work with kids. The woman was shocked when Faith said, "No, I am not, and really don't care to be." But the woman was impressed by her forthrightness; with her and her husband we were to become special friends. Some women don't like women's retreats, sewing circles or singing in the choir. It is not the 11th commandment for her to be involved in any of these. Encourage her to do only what she is sure God asks of her.

3. **Encourage her to fulfill herself.** Does she want to be an artist? A writer? A career woman? Encourage her. Does she want to work outside her home? Encourage her. Does she want to go back to school? Encourage her. Does she want to run the marathon? Encourage her to just do it. A housewife? Encourage her to excel as a housewife. Everyone needs "self-actualization," as Abraham Maslow called it, the need to become what we can become.

4. **With her, find a support person** who understands the ministry and is herself a woman "full of grace." Perhaps she will be another pastor's wife, strong and experienced in the ministry, willing to listen, a person of hope and humor, a woman of prayer.

5. **Share in her spiritual development.** Talk in detail about your own spiritual struggles; discuss about the events during the day that blessed you and at the end of your workday, leave the problems in your church study. Get her a good book to read that seems especially suited to her. (My wife will read anything by J. I. Packer.) Listen, really listen to her feelings, not just her words. Encourage her to use "I" sentences. "I feel very lonely here." "I am confused about my role in the church." "I am depressed today and don't know why." "I've really enjoyed this day and let me tell you why." Pray with her. Ninety-five percent of pastors do not, according to surveys taken.

6. **Be faithful.** At a memorial service recently, the son of the man we honored said, "The only thing Dad wanted another woman to do for him was to point him to Mom." What a tribute! Forty percent of pastors confess to an inappropriate relationship with a woman other than their wives. What a gift it is to a wife for her husband, though he may have failed in the past, to be faithful to her now and to the end of his life.

7. **As you have "issues" that put you at risk. Resolve them.** In a moment you will read Marian's story. She was and is a beautiful lady. She loved her pastor husband and stood with him, though by her own confession, he "had a few issues" that became part of his loss of a pastorate and perhaps the loss of his life. She grieves for his loss, but she, too, lost so much, cried so often, wanted to return to ministry if she could. Her plea is that if there are "issues" in your pastor/husband, (anger, greed, lust, a dominating spirit, self-righteousness, pride, etc.) get him (and

yourself) help, now! Character issues can become lethal at-risk factors and your spouse will suffer as much or more than you do.

CONCLUSION

Your spouse serves with you in the difficult work of pastoral ministry. Stresses that press in on your spouse are real and pastor, you must be there for your partner in life. There are scores of reasons for being all that you can and should be, but one reason is when your marriage is unhappy and nearly broken, you both are at risk of losing everything.

MY STORY—MARIAN, WIFE OF AN EXITED PASTOR.

My story begins when my husband and I were asked by our former pastor and friend to candidate in another state near his church. We had been serving our first church for seven years and after prayer believed that God was calling us to apply. We were accepted and after our move our oldest child entered her first year of college. Our other two children settled into their new school and began making friends. After a year, we took our first vacation, missing only one Sunday. When we got back my husband preached the next day. At the end of the service one of the elders stood up and announced that a special elders meeting was being called for the following evening. My husband attended. Shortly thereafter he returned weeping uncontrollably. He said that we were given thirty days to vacate the parsonage. Sure, he had some personal issues but no one can meet all the expectations people have for their pastor. The most heartbreaking news was that our former friend and pastor was involved in the decision. During the next thirty days my husband preached a few times even though he was battling what we thought was the flu. A congregational meeting was held and I pleaded for mercy with strong cries and tears. But to no avail.

During the next month my husband had a kidney stone attack and was hospitalized. Tests were taken and they showed that his liver was half gone. They gave him only a short time to live. Before my husband passed away our former pastor and his wife came to ask our forgiveness. Within a few months he died suddenly of a heart attack. Within a very few months my husband died, but before he did the elders of the church from which we were so painfully dismissed flew to the bedside of my husband, now in the hospital. They sincerely asked for his forgiveness. We appreciated this, but what sorrow we experienced before his death and then in his death.

My husband was brought up in a very abusive family and he had many unresolved personal difficulties. He also had a very strong personality. God was very gracious to bring him to salvation when he was young. God also gave my husband a true heart for the lost and at our first church he led a convicted murderer to the Lord. Our children went through their own trauma when our family was blown apart. However, God was good. Two became faithful Christians and have good ministries of their own; the third is now a very strong Christian woman after running from the Lord for many years. I serve the Lord at our church as an Altar Minister and am part of the prayer team working with the church's food pantry. During stressful times like these I learned to lean heavily on the Lord. Psalms 27 and 91 have been an encouragement and strength to me. Asking God why is not the answer. Only know that in the midst of conflict God is teaching us to trust Him.

I would encourage any pastor who is in jeopardy of losing his post as pastor to make sure there are no important unresolved matters in his life. Check in with elders and talk over any problems regarding personality or church business issues. Then bring these all before the Lord in prayer. Be willing to be open before the Lord and His people. A humble spirit is of great value. God has been blessing me and my family these thirty years since my husband entered Heaven. I'm now eighty-three years old and attest to the fact that Jesus is Lord indeed and has never failed me. All I can say is, "Satan meant it for evil, but God has used it for good."

CHAPTER 11

When Faith Finds a Testing Place

When the Church is 23 percent mean

Most of us in ecclesiastical work have had a "baptism of fire" somewhere along our otherwise fascinating journey. Mine came in my shortest pastorate. After three and a half years of ecstasy in my first assignment, I had my agony in the second. When I resigned one Sunday morning in June, a little ten-year- old broke out of the church shouting, "My daddy has been hoping for this for two years!" Me too!

Research has found that 23 percent of all churches have forced a pastor to resign. Fifteen percent of these have done it more than once. No statistics for at-risk pastors have been compiled. Studies have shown that as little as three to four leaders in a congregation can prompt a pastor's termination. I say this not to condemn the church but to say you may find that the church becomes a testing place, especially for at-risk pastors.

The "My Story" after each chapter is witness to the fact that the church can be a testing place for its pastors. The best defense, it is said, is a good offense. If you are at risk, you must prepare for the possibility that you will lose your ministry entirely. That preparation (a good offense) is what this chapter suggests.

My faith found a testing place. Sparing you (and myself) the agonizing details of that ministry, I believe to this day that I learned more about myself and the wily side of church work in that experience than I did in years of study in academia. It's true, "the testing of your faith develops perseverance ...that you may be mature and complete..." (James 1:3, 4). Read 2 Corinthians 6:3-10. I know now, as the old after-shave commercial put it, featuring a man slapped in his newly shaved face with a palm- full of the advertised lotion, "Thanks, I needed that!"

Sadder news is that almost 40 percent of those involuntarily exited from the pastorate never return. About 29 percent of them take ten to fifteen months to find another place to serve.

When a crocodile surfaces, its length is measured, it is said. Just as you can know a crocodile's size only when it is taken out of its most comfortable environment, so you know another person's character when that person is taken from where he is comfortable to where he is exposed. When measured by what we are in conflict and turmoil, that we are and little, if anything, more. Scary, isn't it?

Wherever blame is laid for the epidemic of pastors torn suddenly and unceremoniously from their pulpits, neither pastor nor church is excused from a response that is thoroughly Christian and further matures and completes the faith of both. No matter how ugly the exit may be, or what bogus reasons may be given to justify or excuse it or what painful memories it has created, it has been a testing and training place equipping us for the ministry that lies ahead.

To respond well to injustice, false accusations, or to the pain we bring on ourselves, I suggest several affirmations to be tenaciously held and often repeated. You may feel as flat as an empty wallet, on a dead-end road to nowhere, raw as an open wound, but you will live again, if your bottom line has in it biblical affirmations for when the church becomes your testing place. Even if you are not at risk presently, prepare now for the inevitable: serving at risk sometime is the future. You just might protect your future and guard your present by making these affirmations a personal creed, firmly held.

Affirmation 1: Experiencing trial is an inevitable part of life.

In an early translation of 1 Peter 1: 6, the phrase "if necessary" is used in reference to trial. It is a soft way to suggest that trial is necessary, that is, it is as inevitable as it is an indispensable part of life. Certainly this is solid biblical teaching. Job knew well that "Man born of woman is of few days and full of trouble" (14:1). Peter understood that fiery trial is no "strange thing." It is normal to life. Even more for ministers. Matthew 10 uses these phrases applicable to those who serve God: "sheep among wolves," "they will deliver you up," "you shall be hated," "when they persecute you." Thorns are inseparable from the rose; daylight is followed by darkness; life always has death in it. Trouble is an inevitable part of life. You must be prepared to find life hard, even as hard as a forced termination.

Affirmation 2: The trial I experience is temporary at best.

"For a little while" says 1 Peter 1:6. The same idea is found in 1 Peter 5:10. Paul spoke of "momentary light affliction" in 2 Corinthians 4:17. The shock of a pastoral exodus is that it feels like a bloodstain that will never wash out, a desert with no oases, an end with no new beginning. But the past is not the future, the present chapter is not the last chapter, an episode is not the whole story. Your little bark sails a restless sea. Pastors in stress remember, however, trouble is temporary at best.

Affirmation 3: Trial will be of great value to my life.

First Peter 1:7 almost startles us, when in the older translation it reads that the result of trouble will be YOUR praise, glory and honor at the return of Christ. Words usually reserved for Jesus referring to a person tried by fire. If "at the return" seems far off, then read in 1 Peter 5:10,

"After you have suffered . . . He himself will restore you and make you strong, firm and steadfast." Trouble makes us see things more clearly, straightens out our priorities and pushes us forward. As a piece of Haiku poetry puts it, "My barn having burned down, I can now see the moon." You may be pressed down with a load of sorrows. Affirm it, however: Pain and suffering have great value.

Affirmation 4: In trial, I will maintain my personal relationship with Christ.

The sense of 1 Peter 1:8, 9 is that even if trial comes, you have a trust and love relationship with Christ which provides joy greater than can be expressed, though defined by every superlative imaginable. Pastors, especially at-risk and exited pastors, are sometimes angry with God and neglectful of all that maintains their relationship with Him. I have seen it over and over again, the love and trust of a pastor at risk weakens and with it goes the joy. Contemplate the joyous outcome of your faith: salvation. Be not tyrannized by the moment. Let not the pain paralyze your faith. Cling to Him as a branch to a tree. Affirm: I will maintain my personal relationship with Christ, no matter what is happening.

Affirmation 5: In trial I will rule out ever getting even.

Of Jesus it is written, "When they hurled insults at him, he did not retaliate; when he suffered he made no threats..." (1 Pet. 2:23). The temptation, especially when a pastor has been unjustly treated, is to "return the compliment," even the score, give as good as you have been given. You may be as bitter as a Chicago wind in March, but revenge is not yours to exercise. One pastor asked to resign by his elders, threw up all over the congregation the following Sunday. Later exonerated, he gave reason for the elders to require his resignation again for his foul retort when asked the first time. And this time he was forced to resign. Affirm it: All getting even is ruled out.

Affirmation 6: In trial I will commit myself to the God who always does what is just and right.

Of Jesus it is said, "Instead (of retaliation) he entrusted himself to him who judges justly" (1 Pet. 2:23b). The command for us is, "So then, those who suffer according to God's will should commit themselves to their faithful Creator and continue to do good" (4:19). You hand over your honor, your name, your job, your family, your security and your future to the God who judges our situation accurately, who will not allow us to be tried beyond our strength, who will reinforce us by the trouble he permits. Satan will be artful to entrap you, approach you in fascinating guise and will extend to you gilded bait. But before conflict occurs or you are defined as being at risk, make this affirmation: In everything I will commit myself to the God who always does what is just and right.

Let stress, common to the at risk condition, come. We will continue to believe in God even though He may be silent. He is there and always does what is just and right.

CONCLUSION

I suggest this creed for pastors, especially at-risk pastors:

> I Believe…
> Experiencing trial is an inevitable part of life;
> The trial I experience is temporary at best;
> Trial will be of great value to my life,
> Therefore, in trial I will maintain my relationship with God;
> I will rule out ever getting even;
> I will commit myself to the God who always does what is
>   right and just.

May I suggest that you write out this creed and post it, frame it or otherwise keep it close at hand. The church can become your testing place. Would to God that when the trial is over, you can testify, "…when he has tested me, I will come forth as gold" (Job 23:19). You will have protected your future in vocational ministry and guarded your present.

"O that all my distresses and apprehensions might prove but Christ's school to make me fit for great service by teaching me the great lesson of humility." —Puritan prayer

MY STORY—RON

Coming out of seminary I secured a position in a large church in the Bay area as a Children's Pastor. My experience there has come to be viewed as a spiritual Vietnam. Many of our young men who went over there were challenged to their core on what America really stood for and how it was displaying those values to the world. In similar fashion coming straight out of seminary I was naïve as to how the "church" really operates. Expecting to work alongside my fellow pastors for the cause of Christ I was appalled at the politics, backstabbing, and backbiting that I encountered on a routine basis. After serving for two and a half years the senior pastor strongly suggested that I secure my ordination. After completing the process he called me into his office and informed me that it was time I sought my own pastorate and, oh, by the way, "You're not in the budget next year." This was mid-August, my wife was pregnant, we had a house to sell and I had no obvious opportunities ahead of me. I was blindsided, never saw that coming. Shocked, I left his office to discuss with my wife what had just occurred. We were both numb for a couple of days. God walked us through that minefield, but not without some significant scars. Although that crisis happened twenty-eight years ago, only within the last couple of years did I release the remaining bitterness and resentment. Now when I hear of young persons considering the ministry my heart hurts for them and the pain they will most likely endure trying to serve Christ.

CONCLUSION—FINISHING THE RACE

It was the 1968 Olympics in Mexico City. The marathon that year was won by the runner from Ethiopia. The stands soon cleared of those watching the race after the Ethiopian crossed the finish line except for a few who wanted to see the entire race.

Cheers went up from the stands as runner after runner broke through the tape. Then came the last runner, hurt, bleeding, exhausted. It was hours after it seemed the race had concluded. He had fallen but had gotten up to run as best he could. As he crossed the finish line, the few people who remained cheered. The uproar from the almost empty stands sounded as if the whole stadium was still filled, as if he had been the winner. He was the runner from Tanzania… and he was last.

Everyone wondered why he had not quit long before. Reporters rushed to his side as he acknowledged the cheers from the almost vacant stands. They asked him the obvious question: "Why did you bother to continue the race once you had fallen, once you knew you could not win it?" His answer is unforgettable. The exhausted runner, catching his breath said, "My country did not send me 7,000 miles to start the race. They sent me 7,000 miles to finish the race."

Finishing the race is God's gracious intention for you. He has committed Himself to your restoration in these words, "And the God of all grace, who called you to his eternal glory in Christ, after you have suffered a little while, will himself restore you and make you strong, firm and steadfast … Amen" (1 Pet. 5:10).

There is much more to be written. To lessen the at-risk condition, I have offered simple counsel appropriate to each factor. You protect your future in ministry and guard your present by knowing not only what puts a pastor at risk but also what protects you against an unplanned loss of vocational ministry. In conclusion, I list for your thought other helpful preventive and recovery factors not previously explored.

- Minister "on purpose." Have a biblically justifiable reason for what you do.
- Count your blessings. Gratitude is a healer.
- Network now. You will need others.
- Save money. You may need it, if you lose your income.
- Image the church properly.
- Learn to live with some questions. No one has all the answers.
- Practice grace in every situation. Grace begets grace.
- Quit chasing perfection.
- Balance sail and ballast. Sail keeps you moving; ballast keeps you steady.
- Stay within yourself. Be yourself confidently and calmly, especially in the stresses.
- Communicate, communicate, communicate.
- Keep becoming. A better pastor, preacher, person every year.
- Find pleasure in persistence.
- Stay off elevators that take you beyond your competencies.

Lastly, you may wish to take the Pastor-in-Residence At-Risk Pastor Profile found in the Appendix. This tool will help you identify where you are presently on the at-risk continuum.

Both to churches and to pastors let me repeat with conviction and concern: It is a terrible loss to lose a pastor. To the pastor let me say it one more time… Protect your future! Guard your present!

CHAPTER 12

When Risks Lead To Transition, Is There Hope For Renewal?

"Praise be to the ... the Father of compassion and the God of all comfort, who comforts us in all our troubles, so that we can comfort those in any trouble with the comfort we ourselves have received from God."
2 Cor. 1: 3, 4

A missionary friend described how a ministry transition impacted her family's lives for years. "After losing his ministry position, my dad let go of his passion. After more than ten years of dedicated service, he quit following the ministry trail altogether. Eventually, it affected every aspect of his life and led to my parents' separation and divorce. They still talk about the root of their issues beginning when he lost that job and the depression, frustration and despair that followed. I saw how the loss of ministry can have a huge effect as I watched the results unfold in the lives of those I loved growing up. Now, too, in my own family, we have faced the loss of a seemingly clear and specific calling from God and are living through the 'what now,

God?' or 'did I misunderstand?' phase. As I face these issues I want to gain a godly perspective of how to deal with the trauma and transition."

The story is heartbreaking. I wish it was a rare event, but it is all too common in the lives of pastors and their families. Transition in any profession is tough. However, when a pastor is in transition, he often loses his support group, friends, finances, place of residence, and he certainly leaves behind his church family.

For those of us who have been through a forced exit the moments are frozen in time. It's the moment at a leadership meeting, a luncheon appointment, or perhaps a house call when out of the blue you are being asked to step down, to resign, to leave, or you hear the words, "You're fired!" Perhaps you've not heard those words but you sense the need to step down, you feel that all your efforts are making little impact or that there isn't going to be a breakthrough in the ministry, and the only choice is a transition. Whatever the case, when the risks of leadership reach a breaking point, transition often follows. If you are in transition, there is hope.

"Quick someone get a tape recorder. This will be good for Ed when he applies for his next position." Those words came from B.H. at the board meeting when I was let go from an assistant pastor position over thirty years ago. They are as clear and the scene as vivid in my mind today as if it happened last week. The anger, the bitterness, the sense of betrayal and failure, the fear and anxiety that flood your being is almost too difficult to describe. The feeling that God, the church, your friends, and other staff members have let you down can be overwhelming. You wonder if Christian service is worth the cost and if the church has any value in your life. This chapter presents a solution for addressing the heartache and trauma a ministry transition can bring. The process has resulted in restoration of the pastoral family. It's brought new hope, renewed enthusiasm for service, and greater effectiveness in ministry for many exited pastors.

Perhaps you've experienced the risk factors discussed in this book, battled for the cause, fought the good fight, endured the hardships of ministry or given your all only to hear those dreadful words, "Your services are no longer needed." Perhaps you've considered the issues from every angle, sought wise counsel, put ministry before family, schmoozed every leader, done your homework, and brought passion and vision to the task, only to reach the conclusion the ministry wasn't a good fit and your resignation was the best option. Perhaps you've allowed sin to enter the picture and you find yourself needing forgiveness and restoration. Or, perhaps, these are the contemplations reoccurring in your mind.

Studies indicate that between 1,500 and 2,000 pastors are forced to leave a ministry EACH MONTH. One study suggested that 24.7 % of all pastors will experience one or more forced exits during their life of service. Often when I have the opportunity to speak with a group of pastors I ask the question, "How many of you have been forced to leave a ministry because of a firing or forced resignation?" In most cases between 33% and 50% were forced to exit ministry and it has never been less than 25 %. In one study, **40**%, of those exited from ministry, never returned to fulltime Christian service. ***Who wants to be a part of those statistics?*** You feel discarded, unwanted and often like a failure. If you are in that situation, you may be asking the question, "Where do I go from here?"

When it happens, you don't know which church to go to or whether to go to church at all, for that matter. You don't think anyone outside of your family cares. Often your spouse feels like there is no real emotional outlet. You may question if God even saw this coming. Did He really want you at the church that discarded you? Some wonder if they are settling for second best by moving on.

Dry-docked submarine

One of the last diesel powered submarines had an excellent record as an intelligence-gathering vessel. But, after many years of service she was outdated, worn down, broken, and of little use. She was placed in dry-dock and the decision was eventually made to refit, update, and restore her for service. Over the next year or so, a new propeller was installed, new electrical components were added, equipment was updated, and every inch of her was inspected and cleaned for peak performance. Upon completion she performed better, was more effective, and required less effort by the crew. Those who served on her enjoyed the renovations. They were able to accomplish more with better morale in the process. A ship the navy had in mothballs to spend the rest of her days in the quiet waters of stagnation became a marvelous vessel with new life for years of service.

In times of transition a pastor and his family can experience the same renovation on their lives and ministry as the once dry-docked submarine. I've heard the testimonies and watched the process happen. Those who come through the transition with a goal and plan of renewal see God more clearly and experience His restoration deeply. It revitalizes the heart and encourages more effective and enthusiastic service to the King.

If you are in transition, PIR Ministries has a program that was developed just for you! It's been proven time after time. One of the greatest aspects of the program is its impact on the entire family. It's called the Pastor-In-Residence program, or PIR program for short, and is founded on the following principles:

1. Only God can bring restoration and comfort out of the turmoil of a forced exit in ministry.
2. The church is God's instrument for fellowship, accountability, and restoration.
3. The PIR program:
   a. Encourages and supports Christian pastors and their families in the vocational transitions of their lives.

b. Provides spiritual and emotional support and networks exited pastors with refuge (or "safe house") churches.

c. Provides opportunities to resolve conflict.

d. Provides an assessment tool (PRO-D) for understanding God's handiwork in creating an individual's passions, skills, and style (manner in which a person's passions and skills come across to others) The PRO-D measures a person's passions, skills, and style in relation to nine leadership categories in the context of one's work environment.

e. Evaluates honestly God's call on the person's life.

f. Helps to acknowledge there is a redemptive quality to pain. Pain is too valuable to waste. When it is handled in a godly manner, pain provides a deeper understanding of God, His care and His plan. It equips a pastor for greater effectiveness in ministering to those he serves.

While in the program, an exited pastor has the title "Pastor-in-Residence" (PIR), which goes on his resume listing ministry responsibilities performed in the Refuge Church. There is an opportunity for the PIR to raise funds through the church. The program involves the exited pastor and his wife with a support team that ministers to the whole family for six months to a year. The program is future based; that is, the goal is to evaluate the appropriate role of service for the PIR and God's call on his life for future ministry.

Periods of transition are excellent times to regain a new perspective of God and His plan for your life. Like the submarine in dry dock there is value in taking time to re-evaluate, refresh our skills, regain perspective, and refocus on the Lord. The joy of ministry, effectiveness of service, and impact on others is the marvelous outcome for those who take the time.

Study Guide 13 – *Making the Most of a Ministry Transition,* provides an overview of the Pastor-in-Residence program.

CONCLUSION

Life holds no guarantees. The ministry position that seemed the perfect fit when we accepted the call can turn out to be an experience we wished we never had. Each leadership position has its own unique set of circumstances, people, responsibilities, expectations, stress factors, time demands, etc. Add to the mix our own limitations and that of our families. The risks in ministry are far beyond our control and it is not surprising that as the risk factors increase, transitions for pastors take place.

Transition has a price. It takes a toll on those who experience it. The spiritual, emotional, and physical elements are traumatic to say the least. However, there is hope and renewal of passion is not just a dream. It often takes time to rebuild and restore our lives so as to make the best of the trials God has brought our way. The Pastor-in-Residence program is a means by which ministry leaders can find restoration, renewal and new hope for the future.

MY STORY—WAYNE

In a desire to walk more closely with Lord and overcome a temptation in his life, Wayne Smith asked a person in the church to hold him accountable in a specific area. However, that request led to his dismissal and Wayne became the ex-youth pastor of his Church. He and his wife, Mary, were devastated. They had served the church for several years, had seen youth come to Christ and then watched them grow in their walk. They were well liked and respected by the families in the church. Their programs were effective and growing as they taught youth in a myriad of ways. They led mission trips, and held regular events, but Wayne had let his walk with Christ fade and now had a goal to rekindle the flame.

What he expected to be a positive move in that direction caused an exit from ministry in the church and rejection from his friends. They were deeply hurt by the rejection of their church family; they wondered whether church was still relevant for them. Mary felt the pain equally as Wayne and at a deeper level in some areas. In their struggles and concern of what to do, the Smiths considered the Pastor-In-Residence (PIR) program. The program was based in a church in a town nearby with a support team trained by PIR Ministries.

As a part of the program the support team helped the Smiths work through a series of questions from program materials. During the process Wayne served as the volunteer part-time missions pastor within his Refuge Church. The six-month program was renewed for another six months. The ultimate goal of PIR is not necessarily restoration to ministry; rather, as Wayne says, "It's being restored in who you are as a Christian, who you are with your spouse and family, and that internal relationship with God." PIR provided support and an outside perspective while the Smiths worked toward restoration.

At the final meeting about a year after they began the program it was recommended that Wayne return to ministry. "One of the biggest issues we dealt with was the issue of forgiveness, and through the PIR team we were able to receive forgiveness and extend forgiveness," Wayne says. "If you don't forgive, a lot of times bitterness will creep in, take root, and really damage a person … so forgiveness was the key to preventing (negative) emotions from taking strong root in my life and my wife's life, as well."

Epilogue

EVEN THOUGH I HAVE IT COMIN', NOBODY BETTER LAUGH

"Mourn with those who mourn..."
Romans 12:15

In a Christian Century cartoon, the Reverend Will B. Dunn appears with a friend, reading a newspaper. "Have you heard, preacher" the friend says, "your fellow evangelist, Jerry Lee Swagger, had to resign his ministry because of sins of the flesh?" Dunn replies, "Oh no, they got Jerry Lee." Dunn continues his comments, "It's a sad day for all TV ministries when one of our brethren goes astray." "You are very generous, preacher," replies his friend, "after all, Jerry Lee Swagger showed no mercy during your 'mascara scam' troubles." As Reverend Dunn leaves the room, he is heard saying, "But to err is human; to forgive divine," "You are a saint, preacher," declares the friend. In the final frame of the cartoon, however, Dunn is behind the closed door of his house rolling on the floor in laughter, privately gleeful at the thought that someone finally got what was coming to him.

Secretly enjoying the justice of God when it is played out in another's life, quietly gloating over his judgment, taking pleasure when he is chastised, and exploiting the situation for all it's worth. We have all had the opportunity to do just that. Every pastor knows two to four other pastors who have forcefully and suddenly been terminated. Have you ever enjoyed it? You may be an exited pastor yourself… or about to be. You would think the Bible instructs us to conclude, "He made his own bed; now let him sleep in it." Or tells us "It's time he got what was coming to him," or the old translation "He got his comeuppance." Rather than "mourn with those who mourn" (Rom. 12:15), "whoever gloats over disaster will not go unpunished" (Prov. 17:5), or "…you shall not look down on your brother in the day of his misfortune" (Obad. 12).

I offer a brief plea for our brothers and sisters in ministry at risk of losing it all or who have already been summarily exited with no other place to serve. I offer a few thoughts on "shooting our wounded." A short Old Testament book speaks loudly to the subject.

Obadiah, the prophet, writes to Edom about B.C. 845, after the Philistines and others had attacked Jerusalem. The city was stormed and looted, a judgment they deserved, and the people of Edom laughed. Since the two peoples were fraternally (Edom from Esau) and geographically related, brothers were laughing at the misfortune of brothers, one side of the family exploiting the humiliation of the other side.

Arrogance was at the root of such a contemptuous attitude. (Obad. 3) Edom thought of themselves as secluded enough (vv. 3, 4), supported enough (v. 7), smart enough (v. 8). Expressing their self-assured pride, they laughed. Failing to see their own weaknesses, inadequacies and sordid possibilities, out of such smugness they laughed, enjoying another's pain. Such arrogance is the root of reveling in another's pain.

Gloating (v. 12), looting (v. 13), collaborating with enemies (v. 14), all common companions of laughing at another's misfortune.

Every day I have at-risk and exited pastors on my mind.

What grieves me as much as anything else about what has happened to them is the pastor who writes of his brother, "He had it coming; glory to God." Another writes, "Big shot, big church, big fall, big shame. Maybe the rest of us can grow now." In these and others I see a big smirk, never tears for the pain another pastor feels. I see contempt and quiet satisfaction.

First John 4:7 instructs us "to love one another." The love of God defines that love. It is unconditional and sacrificial. No circumstance can change it, no misdeed weakens it, no failure touches it. It expresses the reality of our relationship with Christ. It is not merely good thoughts and pleasant feelings. It is entirely incompatible with "hating his brother or sister" (v. 20) to love as Christ loved, at-risk and exited pastors especially need love like this. Rather than the condemnation there is in laughing.

A large share of the grief pastors forced to resign feel is the response of their fellow pastors. They feel abandoned, alone, out of touch. Few, if any, call. Rarely is there an invitation to attend or participate in cooperative events. It's been likened to having leprosy; no one gets close lest they become victims themselves. Behind closed doors, someone is, at the least, smiling.

As Edom, we will become the victims of our own exploitations, cut down by the boomerangs we first hurled. The winds shift and the dirt we throw is blown back into our own faces. If the principle works for the exited pastor, that we reap what we sow, what makes us think it will not be so for us? A nose in the air ought to smell trouble on the way.

So my last plea is this: People eventually get what is coming to them. Laughing at them is not our prerogative, even behind closed doors. To weep is more appropriate. Offer encouragement and grace. "Therefore encourage one another and build each other up…" (1 Thess. 5:11). Who knows? You may be sitting under a lone broom bush yourself someday.

A representative of Pastor-in-Residence presented the burden of exited pastors to a local ministerial group. Afterwards, one pastor present said, "It's a good thing, but we have too many good things to do to add this to our plate." He brushed off the whole thing with a dismissive wave of his hand.

Six months later, when the ministers met again, the same pastor asked to see the PIR rep after the meeting. Was he interested in starting the program in his church? "No," he said. Continuing, "I want to talk about what you do for exited pastors. Last night I was fired by my church."

Who knows? Don't laugh. You may need tomorrow what you dismiss so easily today.

FOR INFORMATION ABOUT
PASTOR-IN-RESIDENCE (PIR) MINISTRIES, INC.
PIR MINISTRIES
POST OFFICE BOX 80
VILLANOVA, PA 19085
(610) 256-9060
The Rev. Ed Lochmoeller, National Director

PIR MINISTRIES
POST OFFICE BOX 64937
VIRGINIA BEACH, VA 23467
(757) 853-7889
Dr. Calvin Frett, Director

PIR MINISTRIES
4013 Robina Ave
Berkley, MI 48072
(248) 752-3508
Roy Yanke, North Central Director
WEB SITE: www.PIRministries.org
EMAIL: Info@PIRministries.org

"What a spectacular ministry! I saw how the loss of ministry can have a huge effect as I watched the results unfold in the lives of my family members as we all grew up. After losing the ministry job, my dad let go of the passion and quit following the ministry trail he'd been on for ten-plus years. Eventually it affected every aspect of his life and helped lead to my parents' divorce. They still talk about the root of their troubles beginning when that was lost and the depression, frustration and despair set in. Now, too, in my own family, we have faced the loss of a seemingly clear and specific calling from God and are living through the 'what now God?' or 'did I understand?' phase." —Andrea G.

"One of the big issues we dealt with was that of forgiveness, and through the PIR team we were able to receive and extend forgiveness. If you don't forgive, a lot of bitterness will creep in, take root, and really damage a person... so forgiveness was the key to preventing negative emotions from taking strong root in my life and my wife's life, as well." —John, PIR

MY (OUR) STORY—DARLA

My husband was a pastor for eight years in a rural South Dakota church, and was then asked to leave. We had an eighteen-month break where we stayed in the community and my husband worked at a state school for mentally and physically handicapped people while I finished higher education. We applied to various conferences in our and sister denominations ending up for five years in a church in Ontario, Canada. The five years at that church were extremely hard. Having a daughter wanting to graduate from 8th grade was the reason we stayed another year.

We left that church and the ministry under duress, coming back to South Dakota to my family farm where we have been for the past fifteen years. Our first year back we said we would not take any church job for a year, which was a good decision. We did get involved in the church after that, I with women's ministries and my husband on the board of elders. Local family politics heavily ruled that church and after a couple of encounters, we left my home church and spent a year just visiting churches in our community.

We ended up attending a very small Methodist Church in the town where we had lived for eight years while pastoring a country church. A lady pastor led the church of about ten in attendance and closure was a possibility. During the two years that we attended, we prayed that God would do a great work in this little church and small town that we had grown to love all those years ago. The pastor was removed from the ministry entirely when her husband transferred to a new place and she was not given a church. It was very hard on her.

My husband did pulpit supply in a couple of Methodist churches where his preaching was appreciated. Our pastor has asked that he and I take a series of four classes that would enable my husband to be recognized as a lay pastor in the Methodist denomination. So, if in the next six months our church could not financially support a pastor, my husband, along with others, would be able to serve as a lay pastor for the congregation.

In both churches, my husband challenged the people to become active Christ followers. The first church was challenged by my husband to reach people in the community for Christ. That would mean some changes from the way things were done. It didn't go over well, and we were asked to leave. The next pastor succeeded in closing the rural South Dakota church. It didn't need to be that way.

In Ontario, a young man who wanted to be a pastor was consistently criticizing my husband on how he did ministry, causing much division in the church with the young couples. Also, every pastor that had been at that church in the past twenty years had left the ministry after pastoring there… and that includes us.

Now, I won't say that we are perfect people, and that we didn't make any mistakes or did things we shouldn't have done. We were called of God to pastor, however, imperfect or not.

I want to encourage you in this ministry of helping pastors. As you get to know them, are there those that you recommend not go back into the ministry, but serve in another way?

I wish we could have had something like this after both churches from which we were asked to leave. Maybe discerning and caring could have helped us do a better job in ministry.

AN AT-RISK SURVEY

The two major factors that put a pastor at risk are vision conflict and compassion fatigue! This is the conclusion of a thoroughly scientific twenty-nine-page paper on the at-risk web survey taken by over 500 pastors. Jay Spencer, Professor Bruce Winston, and Mihai Bocarnea of Regent University in Virginia Beach, VA, validated the original survey with that of 268 other pastors. They determined pastors are at risk of forced resignation when conflict exists over the vision for the church and the pastor is experiencing signs of compassion fatigue, sometimes referred to as burnout. Given one or both of these factors, it can be said with complete assurance that a pastor is in jeopardy of losing the church he serves.

<u>Vision Conflict</u> reflects the clergy's feelings of disparity between what they expected to happen by answering the call to ministry and the events that actually take place creating conflict about what they believe should be the form and results of their ministry.

<u>Compassion Fatigue</u> is a form of burnout caused by and attributed to, the high level of emotional and physical energy invested in the care of others with little opportunity (maybe other-caused or self-caused) for renewal and rejuvenation.

To get your at-risk score in these two major areas, you can take this abbreviated inventory entitled, PASTOR-IN- RESIDENCE: At-risk Pastor Profile. Instructions for self- scoring are provided with the inventory.

Another survey has now been placed on the web to measure the level of these two key factors for the pastor taking the survey. You will find it on pastorinresidence.org or the Regent University web site. The "Validating a Practitioner's Instrument Measuring the Level of Pastors' Risk of Termination/ Exit from the Church" can also be found on the Regent working paper web site.

We urge all ministry staff, especially seminary and Bible college practical theology professors, to read this paper carefully and share its conclusions with their ministerial students.

Our gratitude goes to Dr. Bruce Winston (former PIR Board Member) and his colleagues for their excellent work.

PASTOR-IN-RESIDENCE:
AT-RISK PASTOR PROFILE

This profile is designed to evaluate a pastor's risk of forced resignation from the church he now serves. Pastors are asked to indicate how often they feel the way suggested by the inventory statements.

Section I

Please read each statement and then choose the number that best represents the frequency of the statement in your life.

	Never				Always
	0	1	2	3	4
I am confused about my major role in the church	☐	☐	☐	☐	☐
I have lost the sense of meaning in my work	☐	☐	☐	☐	☐
I feel overworked	☐	☐	☐	☐	☐
I feel my work is futile	☐	☐	☐	☐	☐
I feel that there are more expectations on me than I can fulfill	☐	☐	☐	☐	☐
I wonder about my calling as a pastor	☐	☐	☐	☐	☐
I feel my work is too demanding	☐	☐	☐	☐	☐
I feel my life is far too stressful	☐	☐	☐	☐	☐
Ministry doesn't bring me satisfaction	☐	☐	☐	☐	☐
Generally, I feel exhausted	☐	☐	☐	☐	☐
I find little joy in my work	☐	☐	☐	☐	☐
I feel I would like to leave the church I now serve	☐	☐	☐	☐	☐
I seriously consider leaving the ministry entirely	☐	☐	☐	☐	☐
I feel my hope for success has not developed	☐	☐	☐	☐	☐
It is very difficult for me to say "no"	☐	☐	☐	☐	☐
I feel my personal relationship with Christ is a real problem	☐	☐	☐	☐	☐

The At-Risk Pastor inventory reports on two factors: Vision Conflict and Compassion Fatigue.

Your total score for Vision Conflict is: ___, out of a possible 40 (questions 1-10)

Your total score for Compassion Fatigue is:___, out of a possible 24 (questions 11-16)

If you scored at or above 10 for Vision conflict or at or above 6 for Compassion Fatigue you are encouraged to contact PIR Ministries for advice at: info@PIRministires.org or 757-853-7889

APPENDIX

SELECTED BIBLIOGRAPHY

Faulkner, Brooks R. *Burnout in Ministry*. Nashville: Broadman Press, 1982.

Freudenberger, Herbert. *The High Cost of High Achievement*. Anchor Press, 1980

Gibson, Barbara G. *Who Ministers to Ministers*. Washington: The Alban Institute, 1987.

Hart, Archibald D. *Coping with Depression in the Ministry and Other Helping Professions*. Waco: Word Books, 1984.

Hoge, Dean R. and Wenger, Jacqueline E. *Pastors in Transition*. Grand Rapid: Eerdmans Publishing, 2005.

Julihn, Caroline. *A Sword will Perce Your Soul: A Journey of Restoration and Healing*. Illinois: Tyndale House Publishers, 2011

Leas, Speed. *Moving Your Church Through Conflict*. Washington: The Alban Institute, 1992.

Lewis, G. Douglas. *Resolving Church Conflicts*. San Francisco: Harper and Row, 1981.

London, H.B. and Wiseman, Neil B. *Pastors at Risk*. Wheaton: Victor Books, 1999.

London, H.B. and Wiseman, Neil B. *Pastors at Greater Risk*. Ventura, Regal. 2003

Maslach, Christiana and Leiter, Michael. *The Truth about Burnout: How Organizations Cause Personal Stress and What to do About It.* San Francisco: Jossey-Bass, 1997.

McIntosh, Gary L. and Edmondson, Robert L. *It Only Hurts on Monday.* Carol Stream, IL: Church Smart, 1998.

McBurney, Louis. *Every Pastor Needs a Pastor.* Marble, CO: Marble Retreat, 1977.

Rediger, G. Lloyd. *Clergy Killers*. Louisville: Westminster John Knox Press, 1997.

Rediger, G. Lloyd. *Coping with Clergy Burnout*. Valley Forge: Judson Press, 1982.

Sanford, J. A. *Ministry Burnout*. Louisville: Westminster John Knox Press, 1992.

Shawchuck, Norman and Hauser, Roger. *Leading the Congregation*. Nashville: Abingdon Press, 1993.

Willimon, William H. *Clergy and Laity Burnout*. Nashville: Abingdon Press, 1989.

Study Guide 1
Introduction

1. If you were asked to describe in just a few words a pastor at risk, what would you say?

   _____

   _____

   _____

2. Using the first name only of an at-risk or exited pastor you know, briefly tell his story.

   _____

   _____

   _____

3. According to Jim Krames, how does a pastor feel when forced to resign?

   _____

   _____

   _____

4. Of the twenty-nine possible elements given for pastors being at risk or forced to resign, what one or two would you put at the top of the list? Why?

   _____

   _____

   _____

5. According to one survey, what are the top stressors that pastors in ministry feel?

_____

_____

_____

6. Discuss the statistics regarding pastors compiled by Shiloh Place. (Page XI)

Pray for your pastor by name.

Study Guide 2
Burnout: Who, What And Where Do You Go From Here?

1. Define burnout. How do you know when a person is burned out? Are you?

    _____

    _____

    _____

    _____

2. Why do you think burnout in pastors has been called "compassion fatigue"?

    _____

    _____

    _____

    _____

3. Do the inventory and score it. Share your score with the group. Any fours or fives? Do others in the group agree with your assessment of yourself?

    _____

    _____

    _____

    _____

4. Of the ten suggested ways to protect yourself against burnout, discuss two that you have a difficult time putting into practice. Why? When?

_____

_____

_____

_____

5. Of the ten suggested ways to protect yourself against burnout, discuss two of them that come easily to you. Why?

_____

_____

_____

_____

Study Guide 3
Burnout— Is The Church Responsible At All?

1. When a church's pastor is burned out, what price does the church often pay?

   _____

   _____

   _____

2. Is the church a pastor serves (his workplace) responsible in any way for its pastor's burnout? If so, in what ways? Do you agree with the conclusion to which the group comes in this regard?

   _____

   _____

   _____

3. Discuss the six causes of burnout according to Maslach and Leiter (in the secular workplace) and how may the church contribute to it?

   _____

   _____

   _____

4. Consider Tom's Story. What, if anything, could the church have done to be redemptive in his case?

   _____

   _____

   _____

5. In the church you attend, which, if any, of these causes of burnout are present?

    _____

    _____

    _____

Study Guide 4
Bummed Out But Not Burned Out

1. Define what is meant by "bummed out."

   _____

   _____

   _____

2. List and discuss each of the five protections against being "bummed out."

   _____

   _____

   _____

   Setting Boundaries

   _____

   _____

   _____

   Being Accountable

   _____

   _____

   _____

   Connecting with and Caring for Yourself

   _____

   _____

   _____

Casting Away Weighty Worries

_____

_____

_____

Enlarging the Joy in your Life

_____

_____

_____

3. Six verses are listed which underscore how joy is enlarged. Pick two and discuss them.

    _____

    _____

    _____

Study Guide 5
Vision Conflict

1. What is vision and why is it important for the church?

    _____

    _____

    _____

2. Discuss what conflict is and what it is not.

    _____

    _____

    _____

3. Is conflict normal to the church and, if so, why? Has it happened in your church and, if so, how was it dealt with?

    _____

    _____

    _____

4. When vision conflict occurs in the church, what should we not do in response to it?

    _____

    _____

    _____

5. When vision conflict happens in the church, what should we do in response to it? Talk about it.

Study Guide 6
Can We Talk?

1. Think about loneliness. Define it. Why do you think that loneliness is a major problem among pastors?

   _____

   _____

   _____

2. Discuss the physical effects of chronic isolation and loneliness. Know anyone who exhibits these effects?

   _____

   _____

   _____

3. Think together about the Toni Morrison's quote, "A friend gathers up all the pieces and gives them back to you in right order." What do you think she meant?

   _____

   _____

   _____

4. What is a support group and do you think a pastor ought to be part of such a group?

   _____

   _____

   _____

5. What would be an ideal pastor's support group?

    _____

    _____

    _____

6. Pray together that, if you are a pastor, you will be able to find or start a support group. Or if you are not a pastor, that you will find a way to encourage your pastor to find or start such a group.

Study Guide 7
So What Do They Want Anyway?

1. Expectations of a pastor are numerous. Name some, particularly as you experience them or your pastor experiences them.

   _____

   _____

   _____

2. Which of the above are valid expectations and which are not? Why?

   _____

   _____

   _____

3. When a pastor is a candidate for the pastorate of a particular church, what would you suggest to him in regard to the congregation's expectations of their pastor?

   _____

   _____

   _____

4. Consider each of the ten words of counsel offered in the book.
   Know Yourself
   Accept Yourself
   Be Honest and Forthright
   Consider a Covenant

Ask

Empower Others

Set Intentional Goals

Listen

Let God Speak in the Expectation of Others

Honor your Predecessor

PRAY

Study Guide 8
What The Role Is Called Up Yonder

1. What roles do pastors often play that are not necessarily primary biblical roles?

   _____

   _____

   _____

2. Discuss the three kinds of role conflict, thinking about them in terms of a pastor.

   _____

   _____

   _____

3. Pastors and churches differ in what they consider to be the most important roles for pastors. Discuss this difference.

   _____

   _____

   _____

4. Eleven roles of a pastor are mentioned in this chapter. In your judgment, what three roles are primary? After these three, name three that you consider secondary.

   _____

   _____

   _____

5. How might you encourage your pastor (perhaps yourself) to give priority attention to the primary roles of a pastor?

_____

_____

_____

Study Guide 9
Listed In "Who's Through"

1. Learning to say "No" is difficult at times. Why?

   _____

   _____

   _____

   _____

2. What does it take to learn to say "No" when it is appropriate?

   _____

   _____

   _____

   _____

3. Skaar tried to please everyone. What would you say to him to help him drop this apparent need?

   _____

   _____

   _____

   _____

4. What do some pastors do to prove that they are hard workers?

   _____

   _____

   _____

   _____

5. What should a pastor do, if his motivation is to prove to his congregation that he works hard?

_____

_____

_____

_____

Study Guide 10
Not The Preacher We Wanted

1. What is preaching? What is good preaching? Who among the preachers you have heard is a good preacher? Why?

   _____

   _____

   _____

2. What is a "call" to be a pastor/preacher?

   _____

   _____

   _____

3. What does a congregation have a right to expect from its pastor as preacher? Why is a pastor at risk when he is "not the preacher we wanted"?

   _____

   _____

   _____

4. Of the seven things about preaching people want and need, pick one and expand upon it.

   _____

   _____

   _____

5. Choose a second characteristic of good preaching and discuss it.

   _____

   _____

   _____

Study Guide 11
A Spouse Ready To Quit

1. Put yourself in the place of a pastor's spouse. What are you feeling? Think about whether these feelings are good, bad or neither.

   _____

   _____

   _____

   _____

2. What are some of the expectations put on the pastor's spouse? If you are the spouse of a pastor, what expectations have you experienced and what have you done about them?

   _____

   _____

   _____

   _____

3. How does a pastor's wife generally find out about the congregation's expectations of her? Were they discussed with the search committee? How should she find out about them?

   _____

   _____

   _____

   _____

4. What stresses have you or your pastor's wife experienced besides
    unwritten expectations? What could you do to take some of the
    stress out of her life? What might you do this week? What should
    the pastor do to relieve her stress?

    _____

    _____

    _____

    _____

Pray for your pastor's wife.

Study Guide 12
My Faith Has Found A Testing Place

1. If you are a pastor and you were once forced to resign your position, share how it happened. If you are not a pastor but you know a pastor who exited ministry under duress, tell what you know about that pastor's experience.

   _____

   _____

   _____

   _____

2. This chapter presents a six-part creed as preparation for and help in times of any trial. Here it refers to the trial of an at-risk or forced resignation experience. The first affirmation is that trial is inevitable. Is it? Why?

   _____

   _____

   _____

   _____

3. Tell about any trial you have had, particularly an at-risk or forced exit trial, and consider how it was of value to your life.

   _____

   _____

   _____

   _____

4. How might you maintain your personal relationship with Christ while undergoing trial?

_____

_____

_____

_____

5. After considering the last two affirmations, repeat the creed together and pray that it will become part of your life.

Thank God for the insights He gave you during this study on Pastors at Risk.

Study Guide 13
Making The Most Of A Ministry Transition

An overview of the Pastor-in-Residence (PIR) program:

1. It is a Church-based program where the senior pastor and the board agree to be a host church or refuge church.
2. Those in the program are called a Pastor-In-Residence (PIR). This title goes on their resume along with the responsibilities performed at the refuge church.
3. Within the church a support team of 2 to 3 couples meet regularly with the exited pastoral couple or pastor.
4. PIR Ministries trains the support team and offers consultation as the program progresses.
5. The PIR's finances are raised outside the church setting. However, we ask the refuge church to add a line item in its budget by which the PIR can obtain support via friends and family.
6. The program lasts six months and can be extended for another six months.
7. The program includes a workbook called Support Team Affirmations and an online assessment called PRO-D. It assesses a person's passions, skills, and styles in relation to nine career value areas in the context of one's work environment.
8. The three resources: Especially For Pastors (a program overview), The General Guide (step-by-step implementation of the program), and Support Team Affirmations (workbooks for the support team).

9. There is a minimal cost for the program, which includes a full set of materials and two PRO-D assessments. PRO-D assessments are also available for those in leadership who would like to develop their leadership potential.

If you are a ministry leader in transition, list three benefits you might gain by going through a program like PIR.

1. _____
2. _____
3. _____

If you are in transition, are you familiar with a church body that would provide a positive atmosphere as a refuge church?

If yes, what is its name and contact information?

Church name _____

Pastor's name _____

Contact information–Phone _____

Email _____

Other _____